HOW DOES THE MIND WORK?

(Economy Edition)
Marvels of the Mind
Part I

Dr. King

Kindle version of this book is also available on Amazon as well as many online stores.

Table of contents

Also by Dr. King

 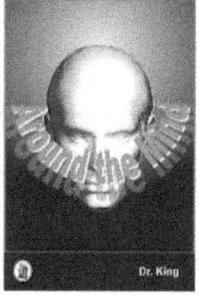

Prologue

The human mind is probably the most complex of the nature's creations. It is an extremely fascinating and intriguing entity, probably beyond the reach of human beings to have a complete understanding.

This book provides an overview of the recent advancements in our scientific understanding of working of the mind. Starting from the fundamentals, the book gradually builds up this most intriguing subject – from simple neurons to consciousness. Making no assumptions about the prerequisites, it unfolds the fascinating story of the mind using simple analogies and easy to understand illustrations. Side by side it broadens the view by comparing the working of the mind with that of a modern computer at various levels of functionality

I have followed a structured approach to cater for the needs of readers with different backgrounds and interests. I have provided the bare minimum details in the running text, and given additional information in specially marked paragraphs. These paragraphs are marked by vertical line on the left margin of these paragraphs. These details can be additional information about whatever was being discussed or in most cases about how a computer achieves the same functionality. If the reader chooses to, these details can be skipped without adversely affecting the rest of the discussion while restricting the scope to desired depth.

For the sake of those who may want to pursue a particular thread of research in greater depth, I have provided a long list of scientific articles picked from research journals and conference proceedings at the end of the book (see **The Bibliography** section).

Apart from providing the readers with latest scientific information about the functioning of the mind, I have another goal for putting these scientific findings in the perspective. In the later parts of this series (i.e. *"How and Why of Yoga and Meditation – Marvels of the Mind Part III"*) on Yoga and Meditation, I am going to use these scientific findings to explain how these seemingly mysterious practices (i.e. Yoga and Meditation) can be explained scientifically.

Overview of the book

This book has altogether 12 chapters other than this prologue and the epilogue found at the end of the book. I have followed a bottom-up approach in explaining the subject – meaning, I start with the most basic things first and take up higher level functionality of the mind as and when we are ready for them.

Chapter 1 and Chapter 2 are basically introductory in nature. In Chapter 2, I have given a rough sketch of how human beings have progressed in the efforts to understanding of the mind, starting from known history to recent times. More elaborate details of ancient efforts to understand the mind are covered in *"Important missing dimensions in our current understanding of the mind - Marvels of the Mind Part III"*. That part also tries to explain why our current scientific understanding may not be complete and why we need to take a lesson or two from ancient philosophy.

Chapter 2 is also important in that it gives descriptions of various scientific instruments that have enabled us in unraveling the mysteries of the mind in recent times.

With these brief introductions, I straight away dive into the subject matter, starting with the most basic component of the mind, namely the neuron. By the way, science views brain and mind as synonymous or two ways of seeing the same thing.

In Chapter 3, I explain the functioning of the neuron in as simple terms as possible. I have intentionally masked technical details and retained only the essentials so that you can focus more on the concepts rather than the intricacies.

A neuron by itself is not very 'intelligent'. It derives its intelligence from working as a group. In Chapter 4 I explain various capabilities of these groups of neurons – or neural networks as they are called – on which the entire functionality of our mind rests.

You may wonder how neural networks come into existence in the first place! Science does not accept the concept of God who could have created them! Chapter 5 explains various ways in which these neural networks come into being and how they dynamically reorganize themselves during the life time of an individual.

After explaining the most basic things – neurons and the networks of neurons, in Chapter 6 I give a very brief overview of the anatomy of the brain. I have intentionally kept this chapter quite light, devoid of too much of anatomical details, so that I don't bog you down with technicalities. Unless you are a student of anatomy, you probably want it that way. But I have covered enough to take us through subsequent chapters.

In the next five chapters, I have covered some of the higher level aspects of our mind namely our ability to perceive things, our ability to remember, our ability communicate through speech, our ability to move, our emotions, beliefs and most importantly our 'free will'. These functionalities are clearly built over the networks of neurons we discussed in Chapters 3 to 5.

As a typical perceptive capability of our mind, I have taken up vision in Chapter 7. Vision is not only the most important mental capability for most of us, but happens to be the most researched upon topic. In this chapter I explain our current understanding of visual processing. I have skipped other perceptive capabilities such as hearing, taste, smell and touch to keep the discussion brief.

None of us can probably survive if we were not endowed with our marvelous capability to remember. Lot of research has gone into this area as well, and in Chapter 8, I summarize these research findings.

One of our mental abilities that make us stand apart from the entire animal world is our ability to communicate through elaborate medium of language. Many animals and birds do have their own language using which they communicate. But our ability to communicate through language is something far well developed.

The language has two aspects – perceiving the speech and producing speech. For the sake of brevity I have skipped speech production and focused mainly on speech perception. Chapter 9 goes into the details of what is involved in understanding the language and how our brain achieves it.

Ability to perform physical action is essential for the survival of most beings. Ability to learn motor skills makes us better evolved beings. In Chapter 10, I touch upon various aspects of physical motion, how they are implemented in our brain, and so on.

Emotions and beliefs make us well suited to survive as a group.

The most essential emotions, that of a mother for her child and that of a lover to his/her mate enable us to carry forward the evolution. We normally term these emotions as very subjective. But scientists try to look at even these objectively. Chapter 11 discusses some of the scientific findings in this regard.

At times our beliefs seem to be doing miracles. Our beliefs can relieve us from several personal and health problems. In chapter 11, I also discuss how scientists explain the way beliefs work.

Most of us consider our 'free will' or the ability to take decisions unprompted, as some unique indication of our being our own masters. But scientists point to some findings that seem to question even this claim. This controversial finding about our mind is still debated. I briefly discuss these controversial research findings in Chapter 11.

The word consciousness has several philosophic and spiritual connotations. As per most philosophers, our consciousness cannot be explained in objective terms. But many scientists try hard to explain that even this apparently subjective phenomenon is just a happening in the brain and nothing else. They try to explain it in physiological terms.

In Chapter 12, I set aside these controversies about subjectivity and objectivity and present a pragmatic view that focuses on the means that enables us have our conscious experiences.

Finally I end the book with an epilogue. In this, I draw your attention to the fact that there are many questions that science cannot answer at the moment. It may not be 'just a matter of time' as many scientists seem to say, but may need a paradigm shift in our current way of thinking and definition of scientific approach itself.

It is definitely within the purview of science to keep an open mind and accept things without bias. In that respect I suggest that we should re-look into the contributions of ancient philosophers and thinkers and take a lesson or two. That takes us to the next part of this series namely *"Important missing dimensions in our current understanding of the mind."*

Reading roadmap

In this section, I will provide you a reading roadmap to make your reading more comfortable and tailored to your needs.

As far as possible I have made sure that the chapters in this book are independent of each others. However, there are unavoidable dependencies forcing a reading order. Figure 0.1 shows possible ways of reading the chapters.

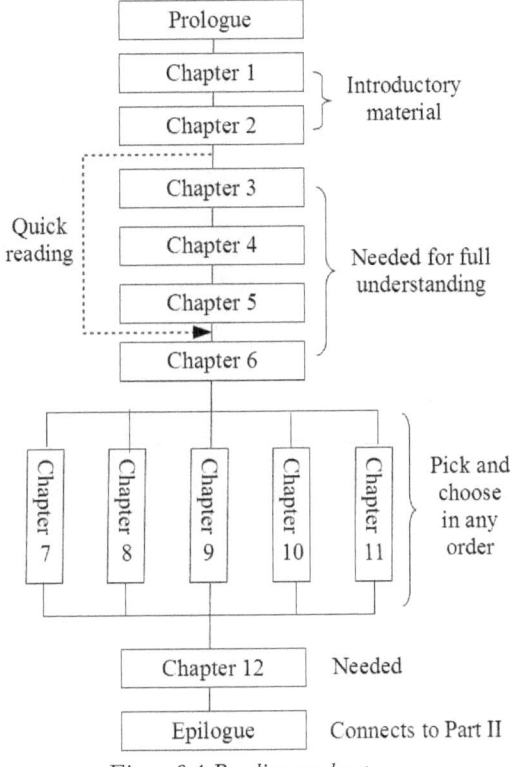

Figure 0.1 Reading roadmap

You have two options. Either you can adopt a two pass strategy or you can restrict the amount you would like to absorb at the macro level.

In a two pass strategy you can quickly read Chapter 1 and 2; skip Chapters 3, 4 and 5; quick read chapter 6; and pick and chose any of the Chapters 7 to 11 in any order; quick read chapter 12 and finally the epilogue. This is the strategy you can choose even in case you are not interested in having a complete understanding of the entire subject but would only like to have a cursory feel.

In the second pass you can read all chapters exactly in the same order as listed in the book, with or without the specially marked details.

Go on with the next chapter where I start with a light introduction. Happy reading!

1 Through Mind we interact with the world

We often think that we interact with the world through our senses and limbs. We see through our eyes, hear through the ears, taste through the tongue, smell through our nose, touch through our skin, and move using our hands and feet. It is true that our senses and limbs are in direct contact with the external world. But what we actually perceive, or the movements we make are through our mind.

Our senses and limbs are like the I/O devices of a computer. We move the cursor on the screen by moving the mouse. But the mouse does not actually move the cursor. Mouse merely says whether we have moved it (i.e. mouse) to the right or left and how much. It is the CPU inside our computer that actually interprets these mouse movements and maps them on to the screen area. It also maps it on to the exact location in a file, say for example, when you are editing a document.

Similarly, the printer does not print your document but it is the CPU once again that decides how to format the document, which fonts have to be used, and finally sends appropriate sequence of commands to the printer to print the characters as and when they are downloaded into the printer.

If the CPU is down or malfunctioning, neither the mouse can move the cursor nor can the printer print anything. Similarly if our mind does not work, say for example we are unconscious or in a coma state, we can neither see, nor hear, nor make any bodily movement. So it is the mind which is behind all our perception and action.

Mind gives us the true picture of the world around us

For most of us who are fortunate to have functioning eyes, our world is mostly visual. But do you realize that our eyes don't convey us the complete information about the world around us?

Firstly, our two eyes see the world through slightly different angles since they are placed at two ends of our forehead. Added to this, our eyes are not identical in shape and other properties. So what our eyes capture is not a single unique image of the world but two slightly different images! It is our mind that combines these two images and provides us a single unique image.

There are other more wonderful things our mind does. The world around is three dimensional, i.e. it has length, breadth and also depth. But our eyes are like cameras. A camera can record images only on a flat film or paper. It cannot capture the depth. Same is true with our eyes. But our mind uses lot of other information to interpret the flat images captured by our eyes and make us feel that we are seeing a three dimensional world.

Our eyes can take only still pictures. Have you ever wondered how then do we recognize movements between objects around us? Once again, it is the mind that puts together various still shots taken by our 'eye camera' and gives us the feeling of moving objects.

It is a good old myth that the moving pictures you see in a movie are because of 'persistence of vision' of our eyes. There is no such thing. Eyes only capture the images frame by frame as they are projected in the movie and it is our mind that makes a movie out of it; and not the eyes!

Our world is not just visual. It has other aspects as well. When we watch a movie on a TV, have you noticed that the spoken words from two individuals talking to each other in the movie, emanating from their respective mouths? But you very well know that there are no sound speaker boxes distributed all over the TV screen. They are only on two sides of the TV. How then the sound coming from these boxes appears to be coming from the mouths of the movie characters that are nowhere near the speaker boxes? This is yet another marvel created by our minds!

Our mind puts together the visual images of the characters displayed on the screen with the sound coming from the speaker boxes, does the necessary 'lip synchronizing' and gives us a feeling that the sounds are actually coming from the images!

You can see the same effect when you watch a 'talking puppet' show. In that case, a ventriloquist cleverly misleads our mind to believing that the sound comes from the mouth of the puppet while in reality, he himself makes these sounds!

It is not just vision and sound but whole lot of other related information that our mind is capable of combining. Though our senses work independently of each other, mind puts together the information they have captured and gives us a true picture of the world around us. Well, almost true picture!

Sometimes, these efforts of our mind to provide us with a true picture can give us a totally wrong picture as well. These are the well known illusions. You probably have visited some of the so called 'Mystery Points' where you see strange things – water moving upwards, things falling down in an inclined trajectory and so on. These are illusions created by clever people to mislead our minds. But for these exceptions, our minds normally provide us with as true a picture of the world as possible.

Mind controls our movements

There are two types of movements – voluntary movements and involuntary movements. We are often aware of how we make voluntary movements. But we may not be so aware of our involuntary movements. But both these movements are orchestrated by our mind – consciously or otherwise.

Our joints, the muscles that move the joints, and so on are almost independent of each other. The complex set of ordered movements of the joints you make when, say you bowl in a cricket game, and need extreme coordination between these joints and muscles. They by themselves are incapable of such a coordinated action. It is the mind that – with or without our knowledge – controls each and every muscle so that the ball leaves the hand at a desired speed, desired direction and makes the desired impact.

Take another example; you are learning how to drive a car. It takes some effort and practice. But when you have mastered it, you drive almost paying no attention to the act. You could be simultaneously listening to music or talking to your co-traveler and so on. But when there is an emergency – a stray animal suddenly crossing the road – we immediately apply the breaks even before we are aware of it. Mind was playing its role not only when you were learning the driving, when you are a skilled driver and also when you are faced with an emergency.

Mind remembers things and does the planning

Sensing events around us and making physical movements is probably done by all living beings. There are other things that make us superior to lower level beings. It is not just sensing things and controlling our movements, our mind does lot of other essential things for us. Just imagine what we would have been if we did not have the ability to remember! Even momentary forgetfulness makes us miserable.

Our mind is like a continuous recorder – 7 days a week, 365 days a year – of happenings around us. Not just recording, but putting together various pieces of information and allowing us to retrieve it as and when we need it. Even a computer cannot match our mind in this respect! Just the voice of some person you know is enough for you to immediately recollect the face of the speaker, his personality traits, your relationship with that person, and so on, even when the person is not in sight!

Our memories are not just repositories of past events. They enable us to perform complex mental operations, planning, creativity, problem solving and so on. Our mind does all this magic! Our thoughts, beliefs, set of ethical rules all have relation to our memory. Memorizing is one of the most important functions of our mind that make our world livable.

Mind makes our world livable

As intellectually superior beings, our bonding with other beings is driven by our emotions, feelings and beliefs. All these finer aspects of human beings owe very much to our minds. Without finer emotions and feelings probably there would have been no difference between us and other animals.

Beliefs, whether religious or driven by social values, enable us to live amidst uncertainty. Most of our beliefs may not correlate with our past experiences but are gradually built up due to the psycho-social environment around us. There are cases when our beliefs can even protect us in the event of emergency and self heal some of our ailments.

There is an old Indian saying that "it is the mind that is the moti-vator, the tool as well as the one that accomplishes things". Our world without our mind does not exist!

Having said all this, we should admit that not all aspects of the mind or how exactly it works, is known to us as yet. We are still in the process of unraveling this mystery.

In the subsequent chapters, I am going to take you through a highly enthralling journey - a step by step process of understanding this marvelous mind of ours. Let us start with the means that enable us to know the mind in the next chapter.

2 How do we get to know about the Mind?

The mind has always fascinated ancient intellectuals and philosophers. Thousands of years back philosophers from Greece, India and probably many more regions had pondered over what mind is.

Ancient Indians even devised various ways to modulate the mind and take it to new heights and perform feats that it is normally not capable of doing. This effort took shape as Yoga, meditation and so on, that we know today.

How did the quest for understanding the mind start? Let me go briefly into the chronological tour of this interesting pursuit of mankind from ancient times.

Understanding the mind through metaphysical means

This approach was followed by most ancient people whether it is the ancient Greeks or the ancient Indian Buddhists and Vedic seers. The Greeks had their own conceptual models of how the mind operated. The ancient Buddhists had elaborate theories about the mind and its working. The Vedic Indian gave an altogether spiritual interpretation of the mind.

These people had no physical means to understand the mind. They either used pure reasoning or the insights gained when their mind was in super conscious state. It will be categorically incorrect to brand their contributions as purely speculative as some modern scholars tend to do.

Greek philosophers like Pythagoras, Plato and others emphasized on reasoning to understand the mind. So also did the ancient Sänkhya philosophers from India. For them, our sense perceptions are too inadequate to know the reality and they can even be misleading.

On the other hand, ancient Buddhist and Vedic philosophers rejected even reasoning as a means to understand the ultimate truth. They accepted only the insights gained when their mind was in super conscious state. These philosophers gave high importance to mind and its functioning. They looked at the mind as an ultimate way to freedom.

I have given a broad sketch of these extremely enthralling philosophical pursuits of ancient Greeks and Indians in "*Important missing dimensions in our current understanding of the mind. - Marvels of the mind Part II*". In the current book however, I will focus mainly on modern approaches to the understanding of the mind.

Empirical approach to understanding of the mind

Probably it was Greek philosopher Aristotle who laid the foundation to empirical approach. He emphasized on keen observation based on experimentation. A series of philosophers and psychologists from all over the world succeeded Aristotle.

The early psychological approach was to observe stimulus-response characteristics of the mind and build a suitable theory to explain the findings. The mind was seen more as a black box and was studied from outside – as if.

Modern approach to understanding the mind is a multi-disciplinary approach involving behavioral psychology, physiology, cellular biology, neuroscience, genetics, and computer science among others. In this book I will mainly focus on these approaches and more so on neuroscience driven approach.

The modern science views the mind either as synonymous to the functioning of the brain or as something that emerges as a result of the functioning of the brain. Or in other words, the mind is the 'brain in action'. To understand how the mind works, we need to understand how the brain works.

Early discoveries about the working of the brain

After the black box approach of the behavioral psychology, came the physiological approaches that resulted in many of the early discoveries about the functioning of the mind. These apparently simple observations provided a peep into the brain and its functioning. The general approach can be summarized as follows.

1. Identify a certain region of the brain that is either damaged or had to be surgically removed as part of a treatment for some ailment.
2. Observe the effect of such damage or removal on the behavioral traits of the person.
3. Conjecture that the damaged or removed brain region was responsible for the change.
4. Confirm this conjecture either by making similar observations on many patients under similar conditions, or by performing similar surgeries on experimental animals.

These studies are called lesion studies. Whether it is the early work on memory, or visual processing, or speech perception and production, or motor functions, all these had lesion studies as their starting point. We will see some of these in later chapters.

Lesion studies were the only option in an era in which no instruments were available to observe a live brain. But as science progressed, newer and newer gadgets were discovered that enabled scientists to 'look into' a live brain without damaging it or hoping for a pre-damaged brain.

One such early gadget that is still being used for diagnostic purposes is the so called EEG machine. This machine works on the observation that our brain emanates electrical signals and these signals correlate with the activities of the brain.

Understanding the brain by monitoring its electrical activity

Our current understanding of the brain is that it is a complex structure comprising of trillions of cells that interact among themselves and the rest of the body through electro-chemical signals. One way to understand the working of the brain is to understand these electro-chemical signals.

Any electrical signal has amplitude - a voltage of specific magnitude, and a frequency - the rate at which this voltage changes from time to time. For example, the electricity in your homes normally has 110 Volts amplitude and 60 Hz frequency (it could be country specific and could be 230 Volts and 50 Hz in some countries).

The voltage generated in our brain is of very low amplitude – of the order of few mill volts (thousandth of a volt) and the frequencies could be something of the order of a fraction of a Hz – that means it takes more than a second to change – to few tens of Hz – that means that it changes tens of times every second.

How are these brain signals measured?

Just like an electronic technician who uses a voltmeter or oscilloscope to measure electrical signals at various points of an electronic gadget, the electrical signals emanating from our brain too can be measured and monitored. By knowing the way these electrical signals change over a period of time, we can have a rough idea of what is going on inside the brain.

Figure 2.1 shows some sample signals emanating from our brain and corresponding frequencies and mental states. These signals are monitored by attaching probes on the surface of the head, and by using a machine called Electro Encephalography (EEG) machine. The first EEG machine was discovered sometime in 1924 by an Austrian psychiatrist named Hans Berger. Figure 2.2 shows EEG recordings being made using an EEG machine.

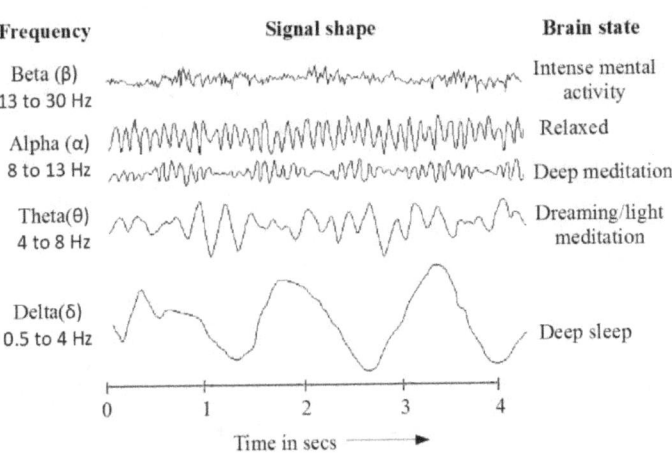

Figure 2.1 Some brain signals and their interpretation

It should be noted that the signals measured from outside the skull by an EEG machine, only give an overall picture, sort of averaging the signals that emanate from various functional units inside the brain. They don't say much about individual signals.

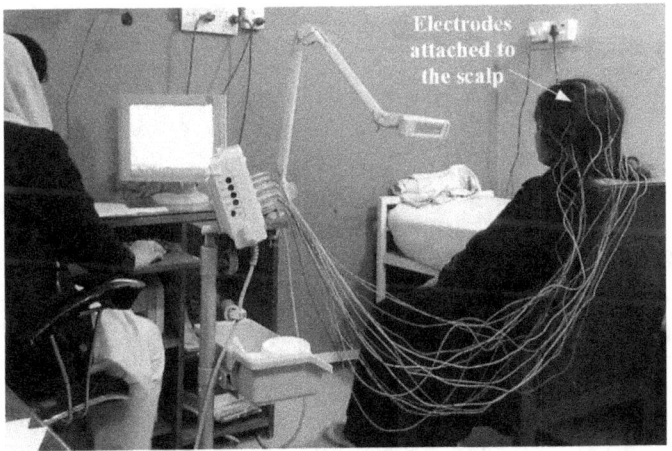

Figure 2.2 EEG being taken

To record individual signals inside the brain, we need to implant electrodes deep inside the brain. This needs surgical intervention and has ethical issues involved when it comes to doing such an operation on human beings. So, normally such measurements are done on experimental animals.

Modern techniques can even record the signals from a single cell or a group of related cells, giving highly accurate data. In rare cases where electrodes had been previously implanted in the brain of human beings as part of some other treatment, such electrodes are also used to record internal signals.

Apart from measuring signals from live brains, brain slices from experimental animals have been cultivated on a grid of electrodes to record the electrical activity among various cells in such slices that are artificially kept alive by immersing them in special medium.

These recordings do give us some idea about the electrical activity in the brain. But these do not give anatomical details of insides of a live brain.

We normally use X-rays to "see" inside the body. We can take photographs of the bony structure inside our body. But internal organs of the brain are comprised of soft tissues that cannot be precisely captured using X-rays. How do we then go about taking photographs of the inside of a live brain?

Nuclear physics based methods to peep into the brain

The next important inventions in the means to peep into the brain were the instruments that were based on nuclear physics. These instruments opened a new chapter in the understanding of the mind. These instruments were used both for diagnostic purposes as well as the study of the functioning of the brain. Let us see some of these instruments.

The PET scanner

An early notable invention was the Positron Emission Tomography (PET) scanner. In this technique the patient is injected with some radioactive substance. As the radioactive substance travels all over the body through the blood and reaches the brain, different brain tissues absorb radioactive substance and later emit different amounts of radiations comprising of Positrons.

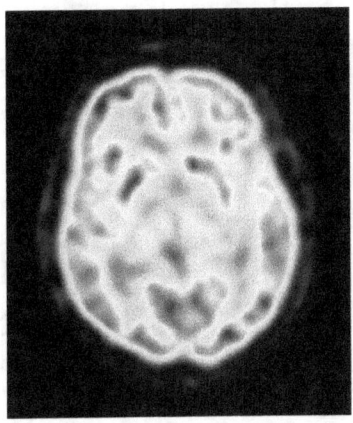

These Positrons get ultimately converted into photons and these emissions of varying intensity are captured to take a picture of the inner brain tissue. Since different tissues emit different amounts of positrons, the intensities of the glow in a PET image changes corresponding to the tissue that has emitted Positrons as shown in Figure 2.3.

Figure 2.3 A PET image

But a PET imaging has some disadvantages. Firstly it requires the use of a radioactive substance. Secondly, the imaging procedure is time consuming and needs multiple scans.

In the early 1980s another method, also based on nuclear physics, appeared on the scene. This method used no harmful radioactive substance nor did it take lengthy time to take the brain pictures. This method was called Nuclear Magnetic Resonance Imaging (NMRI), which was later on called simply Magnetic Resonance Imaging (MRI) to drive away the 'Nuclear' ghost!

An MRI scanner

A Magnetic Resonance Imaging (MRI) scanner that is shown in Figure 2.4, works on the principle of magnetic resonance. The basic idea is as follows.

The subatomic particles in various tissues in our brain act like tiny magnets since they are charged particles spinning all the time. Depending on the exact composition of the brain tissue, these tiny magnets have different strengths.

First these magnets are 'aligned' by applying a powerful magnetic field. Once they are aligned, their alignment is changed synchronously by bombarding them by radio frequency (RF) waves. These tiny magnets 'resonate' at a particular frequency of the RF waves by absorbing maximum energy from them.

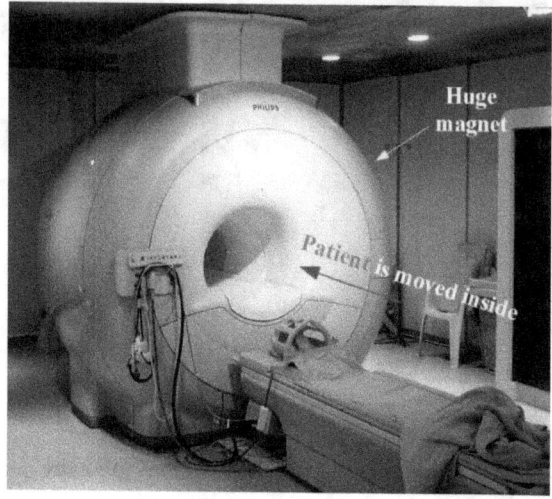

Figure 2.4 An MRI scanner

After sometime, when these tiny magnets go back to their original orientation they emit back some of the energy they absorbed from the RF waves. This amount of energy depends on the frequency of the RF waves, the composition of the tissue comprising of those tiny magnets and the strength of the magnetic field. Based on this emitted energy, the MRI scanner can construct a detailed image of the brain tissue that was involved. A typical MRI image of the brain is as shown in Figure 2.5.

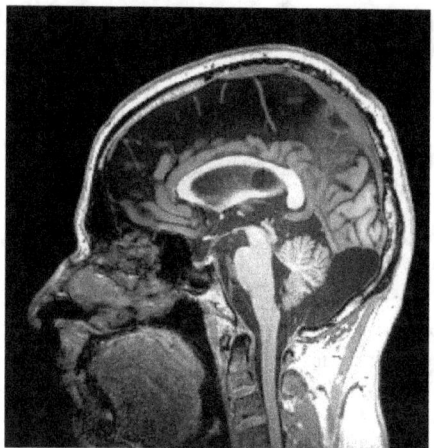

Figure 2.5 An MRI scanned image

As can be seen from the figure, an MRI scanner provided minute anatomical details of the inside of the brain without having to cut open the brain.

But this is not sufficient to understand the dynamic functioning of the brain. For that, we need to get pictures of the brain 'in action'.

For a given task we would like to know exactly which brain regions get activated and in which order. This is what is achieved by a functional MRI (fMRI) scanner.

An fMRI scanner

A functional MRI (fMRI) scanner works almost under the same principles as a normal MRI scanner except that it targets areas of the brain that are active while performing a given task.

How is the activity indicated? When a certain part of the brain is active, it consumes more energy. To provide this energy, more blood flows into that region. Blood has deoxyhemoglobin that has paramagnetic properties. The variation of this deoxyhemoglobin in the regions where there is more blood flow alters the resonance property used by the MRI scanner.

So, by appropriately tuning the parameters at which the MRI scanner works, it can be made to take the images of only those regions where there is increase in blood flow, or in other words there is activity.

This kind of activity – function - dependent imaging helps us in knowing the regions of the brain that are involved in a specific mental function.

For example: what are the brain regions involved when the brain processes a visual image?, what are the regions that take part in producing speech?, and so on. Normally, each of these activities can have multiple phases and by taking a series of scans at appropriate intervals we can even make a 'movie' of the entire activity, if needed!

An fMRI scanner, though provides us the functioning of various regions of our brain while performing various tasks, it only gives a 'macro' level picture. It does not tell us what exactly happens within each of these regions.

As we see in later chapters, each of these regions is made up of networks of neurons that are interconnected in a complex fashion. At the moment, we have no way to visualize the exact way these neurons are connected. Nor we have exact idea of how these neural networks work. How do we progress further?

The advent of sophisticated computers has come to our aid. Using computers, we can make further progress in our understanding of the working of the brain even to the level of neural networks.

Neo-speculative way to understanding the mind

This seems to be the approach that is becoming more and more common these days. This has been made possible by the sophisticated computers that are available today. I call this approach neo-speculative since it basically involves the following steps.

1. Make some observations about the functioning of some part of the brain. Study how it responds to a set of stimuli.
2. Make an informed guess about how that part is working internally. Build a theory explaining the possible way of its functioning.
3. Build a 'computer model' of this part based on the theory. This model may include mathematical expressions capturing various aspects of the model and/or step by step detail of functioning of the part.
4. Implement this model on a computer. Implementation means writing a computer program that mimics the working of a physical system. Such programs are called simulators.
5. Test this computer model with the set of stimuli (actually, the computer analogs of the stimuli) that were used in studying the part under observation and see whether the model responds the same way as the part under observation. This process is called computer simulation.
6. If the simulation succeeds – that means if the responses match, assume that the theory is correct.
7. Accept the theory as correct explanation about the working of the part unless proven otherwise later on.

8. When proven wrong, either refine the model, or reject it altogether and work on a new model.

9. Repeated cycles of this process hopefully move us forward in our understanding of the mind.

Many of the recent advances in our understanding of the mind are based on this kind of simulation studies. They provide very useful insights but their role is always tentative.

Often it is seen that two or more theories, though divergent in details, seem to explain the functioning of the same part, both passing simulation trials. This raises lot of debate among rivaling groups that put forth these theories. One of them may survive in these debates. Often there is also an attempt to unify them in some way.

Whether this kind of speculative approach is the only way or whether it is a temporary solution to our current technological limitations – only time will tell.

Bottom up approach to understanding the mind

In all the approaches I discussed earlier, we started at a higher level and gradually went down deeper step by step in the process of understanding the mind. We started with behavioral traits of an individual, went on to investigate the states of the brain when it is performing various functions, we went further down to look into which regions of the brain took part in these functions and finally how these regions interact with each other and implement the dynamics of our mind. This is a top down approach.

Alternatively, we can take a bottom up approach, starting from a single cell in the brain, understand how this cell functions, how it interacts with other cells, how a group of cells work together, how several such groups cooperate in achieving the functionality of our mind, and finally how the brain as a whole works exhibiting its typical characteristics. This is called the bottom up approach. Several recent developments in cell biology have made key contributions in this regard.

When it comes to explaining the functioning of the mind, it is easier to understand if we take a bottom up approach. And that is the approach I am going to take in this book. So, in the next chapter I will start with the most elementary component of the brain, a cell or the *neuron* as it is called.

3 Neurons: Mini biological wonders

Before I start talking about what a neuron is, let me start with some mundane things.

Look at a building. It could be the house where you live in. It could be your place of work. It could even be the White House or the famous Taj Mahal. What is common between all these?

They are all built using bricks. It is true that they all have many things other than just the bricks. They may have wooden doors, windows; tiles on the roof, and so on. But the 'basic building block' in all these structures is the brick. There could be different types of bricks. Their sizes and compositions may vary. But they are the basic building blocks.

Now-a-days, we all use computers so heavily. Not just computers, but whole lot of other electronic gadgetry. What do you think is common between an electronic watch, a cell phone, a laptop computer and a supercomputer?

They are all built using the same building block namely a transistor. A transistor inside a computer is so tiny that we cannot even see it with our naked eyes. But it does all the wonderful things – calculating, drawing figures, remembering whole lot of things, and so on.

Now let us look at our own body. Each one of has a unique body. And each body has external as well as internal organs, skin, hair, and so on. But all the bodies, no matter how different they are, are all made up of cells. Cells are the basic building blocks that make our bodies, no matter how big or small.

Neurons are the basic building blocks of our brain

As I said, the basic building blocks of our bodies are cells. Neuron is a special cell that makes up our brains. There are as many as 100 billion of neurons in our brain! All of them together contribute to our intelligence, knowledge, experiences, memories, emotions, feelings, phobias, beliefs, biases, and so on.

In other words, these are workhorses behind our mind. Our mind is something that emerges as a consequence of the combined action of all these billions of neurons.

Compared to the enormous complexity of our brains considered as a whole, each neuron is relatively a simple structure.

Figure 3.1: Structure of a simple neuron

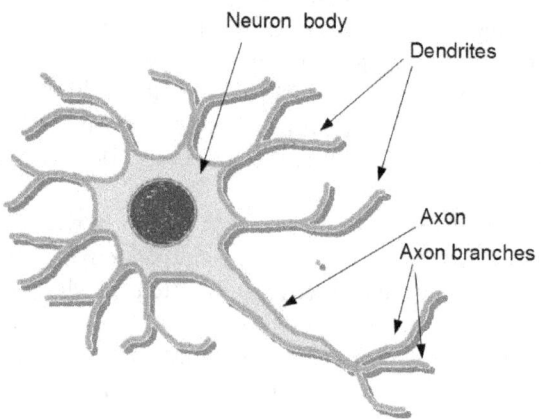

As can be seen in Figure 3.1, a neuron has a cell body, several hair like structures — called dendrites - emanating from the cell body and a single long tube like structure — called axon — extending from the cell body. This axon may branch at the other end into several braches called axon branches. A neuron is so tiny that you can fit as many as half a billion of them in 1 cubic inch of space! But their capabilities are amazing. Their strength is more in what they can do together than as individual cells.

A simple model of a neuron

What does a neuron do? Simply put: a neuron just fires! It is from this firing of billions of neurons, what we recognize as 'the mind' emerges. Of course, this firing has to be in a coordinated way. How do these neurons function together? Before we get into those details, let us first understand how a single neuron functions. Instead of pouring out whole lot of technical nitty-gritty, I will try to explain the functioning of the neuron using a simple day-to-day example.

Figure 3.2: A bucket kept under a dripping tap

Consider a bucket with some water in it, kept under a dripping tap as shown in Figure 3.2. The water trickles down into the bucket as tiny drops and gets collected. After sometime, the bucket gradually fills up. The collected water overflows when the water level in the bucket reaches the rim of the bucket. Once this happens, any more drops that trickle down have no effect unless you empty the bucket. Once the bucket is emptied, the whole process repeats.

Now, instead of a single tap, let us consider a case with three identical taps adding identically sized drops into the bucket. Now the bucket gets filled three times as fast, as compared to the previous case. More the taps, faster the bucket fills and faster the water reaches the rim or 'the threshold' as we call it. Once it reaches the threshold, the water overflows. Instead of three taps, we can have a single big tap that adds three times the amount of water into the bucket as compared to the initial smaller taps.

Figure 3.3: Bucket filled by several taps of different sizes

In general, we can have one or more taps, each with a different size as shown in Figure 3.3. The amount of water that gets added to the bucket in such a case is the sum of water added by each tap.

The water overflows when the added water reaches the rim of the bucket or the threshold. If there are three taps, the first adding some amount of water every time, the second adding twice that amount, and a third one adding three times the amount added by the first one, then the total amount added each time by all the taps put together is 1+2+3 = 6 times the amount added by the first tap. The same amount could have been added by having 6 identical taps each the size of the first one. In that case the total water added each time would be 6 * 1 = 6.

In other words, the amount of water added is equal to the sum of the amounts of water added by each tap, which in turn depends on the size of the tap. When this added water reaches the threshold, the bucket overflows.

Where does this simile fit with the neuron we are talking about? This is as follows.

The body of the neuron is like the bucket in the previous example. The dendrites are like the inlets to this bucket. Electrically charged particles – called ions - that flow through these dendrites into the cell body are like the water drops dripping from the taps. These charged particles increase the electrical voltage inside the body when they get accumulated. The neuron 'fires' when this voltage reaches a threshold, just like the water that overflows when it reaches the rim of the bucket. What exactly is meant by 'firing' of a neuron? Firing means a surge of electrical current from the neuron body through its axon.

Now, as I said earlier, a neuron may have one or more dendrites. And each of them can input variable amount of electrical charges into the neuron body. The voltage inside the neuron body can be viewed as the sum total of electrical charges arriving through each dendrite – very much similar to the drops of water falling into the bucket from one or more taps.

From where do these electrical charges or ions get into the dendrites? They are injected by the axons of other neurons that are connected to the dendrites through contact points called 'synapses'. The neuron whose axon is connected to the dendrite of another neuron through a synaptic contact is called 'pre-synaptic neuron' and the one to whose dendrite this axon is connected is called 'post-synaptic neuron'.

Figure 3.4: Pre and Post synaptic neurons

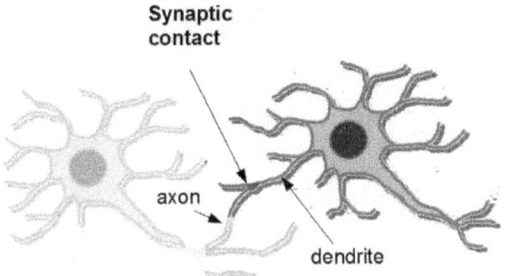

When a pre-synaptic neuron fires, the electric current that flows through its axon reaches the synaptic contact. At the synaptic contact, this electrical energy gets converted into chemical energy, which triggers transfer of electrically charged ions into and out of the body of the post-synaptic neuron. This flow of ions into and out of the post-synaptic neuron body generates electrical voltage inside its body. This is quite a complicated phenomenon. I will skip those details here.

The post-synaptic neuron fires when this internally generated voltage reaches the threshold. That is, at that time, there would be a surge of electric current that shoots out from its axon. Due to the internal ion transfer mechanisms this surge will be in the form of a spike that shoots up and dies down after a short gap of around 1 millisecond. This spike moves down the axon at a speed of few hundreds of feet per second and triggers another neuron to which this axon is connected, and the whole chain of action continues.

There could be one or more pre- synaptic neurons whose axons are connected to one or more of the dendrites of a post synaptic neuron. Each connection is established through a synaptic contact. The 'strengths' of each of these contacts may or may not be the same. More the strength, they can induce more voltage into the post- synaptic neuron. Since each of these synapses tries to fire or excite the post-synaptic neuron, these synapses are called excitatory synapses.

Coming back to our bucket analogy, the number of synaptic contacts made on one or more dendrites are like the number of taps that fill the bucket. The synaptic strengths are like the sizes of the taps. This analogy is very close, but does not explain complete capabilities of the neurons. To explain some more interesting phenomena that happen in the neurons, let me slightly extend the bucket analogy.

A more realistic model of a neuron

Figure 3.5 Bucket with taps, siphon and leakage

The neuron described in the previous paragraphs highlights only one aspect of a typical neuron, that is, it can trigger another neuron to fire. As we see in real life, life is full of duals. It is intuitive to expect that a neuron must also have the ability to 'inhibit' another neuron from firing. Further, a neuron being a biological device, we expect it to have decay, fatigue and so on. I will now explain these aspects of the neuron by extending our bucket analogy a bit.

As before, consider a bucket kept under a set of dripping taps, each tap adding same or different amount of water to the bucket depending on the size of the tap. These taps together help in increasing the water level and eventually make the bucket overflow when this level reaches the rim or the threshold.

Let me add one more device to this bucket, Assume that a siphon is plunged into the bucket, which depletes the bucket drop at a time as shown in Figure 3.5

Once again, let us assume that the amount of water depleted by the siphon is proportional to its size. Bigger the siphon more will be the water drained. In effect, the siphon tries to bring down the water level as against the taps that try to do the other way. The role of the siphon is to inhibit rising of the water level.

Let me add some more twists to this bucket analogy. Assume that there is hole somewhere near the bottom of the bucket as shown in Figure 3.5. This hole, drains the water in the bucket in small quantities till the water level goes below the level where the hole exists.

In effect, left to itself, the water level in the bucket is kept constant at a level which I have marked as 'minimum level' in Figure 3.5.

Since the siphons are fitted in such a way that they cannot drain the water below this level, the bucket is guaranteed to have water up to this minimum level. With this leaky bucket with some set of dripping taps and some set of draining siphons, we have the following scenario.

The dripping taps try to fill the bucket and make it overflow. But they have to compete with the rate at which the water drains out through the leaky hole in the bucket. The siphons too try to bring the water level down and prevent it from overflowing.

Now with this interesting setup, whether the bucket overflows or not depends on who wins the race – the dripping taps or the siphon combined with the leaky hole.

Mapping this analogy to our neurons is quite straight forward. The dripping taps are the excitatory synapses connected to the dendrites of the neuron. The siphons are the 'inhibitory' synapses connected to the dendrites of the same neuron. The leaking hole is leaky nature of the neuron that tends to lose its internally stored charge over a period of time till it reaches a minimum level.

As with the bucket, the combined effect of these synapses is realized by summing up the strengths of excitatory synapses and subtracting the sum of the strengths of the inhibitory synapses. Of course, we need to subtract the loss due to the leaky hole as well. But since this leakage is quite small, we ignore it in most of our discussions, even though at times it can play a crucial role as we will see later.

The only other thing we left out is the water level corresponding to the rim of the bucket. In the neuron, we call it a threshold, some voltage that has to be reached before the neuron fires. In practice, this threshold is more or less fixed, but we assign arbitrary values to it to simplify our discussions.

In this section, I used the bucket analogy to explain the working of a neuron in conceptual terms. But the details of the actual working of the neuron are quite complex and we are yet to know all the details.

You may be wondering as to how exactly a neuron is made to fire by a pre-synaptic neuron. Now, I will give you a brief overview of this process which you can skip if you like.

Actual working of a neuron

As I said, it is the axon of the pre-synaptic neuron that excites or inhibits a neuron from firing or otherwise. The axon achieves this by the chemical changes that take place at the synaptic contact through which it connects to the dendrite of the post-synaptic neuron.

Let us consider excitatory synapses and see what happens at the synaptic contact. Refer to Figure 3.6 which shows a synaptic contact made at the dendrite of a post-synaptic neuron. The electrical energy travels along its axon when the pre-synaptic neuron fires. A series of events take place when it reaches the synaptic contact. Let me consider the simplest mechanism (there are many more).

Synapses have what are called vesicles that store substances called neurotransmitters. There are different types of neurotransmitters, each working in a specific way.

When the electrical energy reaches the synapse, these vesicles get stimulated to release the stored neurotransmitters. These neurotransmitters come out of the synapses and reach the dendrite body as shown in Figure 3.6.

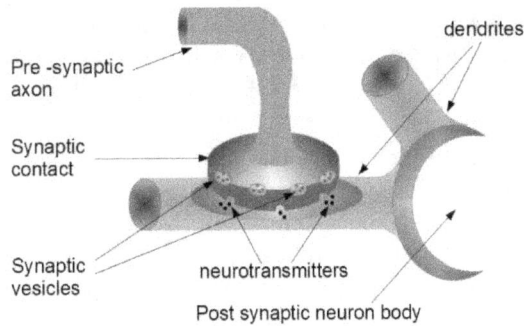

Figure 3.6: A pre-synaptic neuron trying to excite a post-synaptic neuron

The dendrite surface has what are called 'ion channels' that are normally closed. One typical sequence of events that follow is as shown in Figure 3.7.

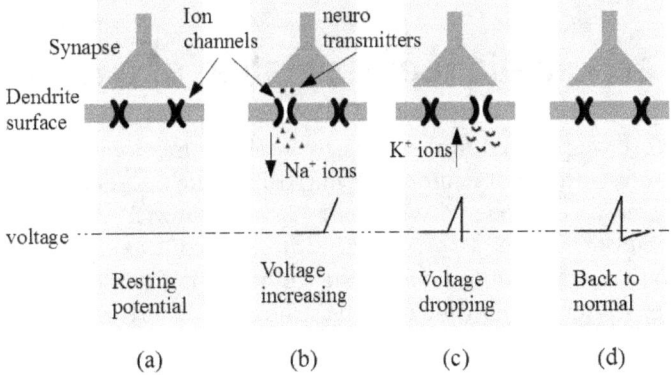

Figure 3.7: One typical set of events that happens before a neuron fires

To start with, the post synaptic neuron is at its resting state with its internal voltage in at what is called 'resting potential' as shown in Figure 3.7(a). In this state the ion channels are closed.

The neurotransmitters released from the synapse open up some of the ion channels that allow Sodium ions (Na+) to flow into the post-synaptic neuron as shown in Figure 3.7(b). As a result of this ion flow into the neuron, the voltage inside the neuron increases till it reaches a threshold (often referred to as 'action potential').

When this threshold is reached, another set of ion channels, that are controlled by voltage, open up and the previously open Na+ ion channels close. Now Potassium ions (K+ ions) start flowing out of the neuron through these newly opened channels as shown in Figure

3.7(c). This flow of ions in the reverse direction brings down the voltage. The decrease continues till it reaches slightly below the resting potential. At that time, even the K+ ion channels close.

There are other mechanisms in the neuron that gradually bring the voltage back to the normal level as shown in Figure 3.7(d). This is how a 'spike' is generated when a neuron is excited by a pre-synaptic neuron. And this spike travels down the axon of the neuron that just fired.

The story does not end there. After several such firings, the neuron could lose all its K+ ions and would have excess Na+ ions. In this state, the neuron cannot operate any more. There are other mechanisms called 'ion pumps' that restore the ion levels inside and outside the neuron so that the neuron is once again ready to get excited.

A schematic representation of a neuron

Before we proceed further, let us completely move on to the discussion of working of neurons, leaving behind the bucket analogy which has served its purpose. We need a concise pictorial representation of a neuron with its associated dendrites, synaptic contacts, the threshold, and finally the axon. In the forthcoming discussions, I will use the representation of the neuron as shown in Figure 3.8 below.

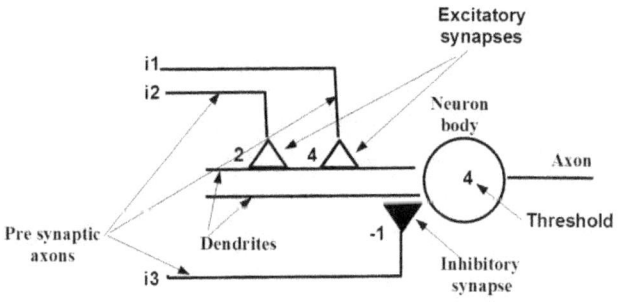

Figure 3.8: Schematic depiction of a neuron

In Figure 3.8, the circle represents the body of the neuron. The number written inside this circle indicates the threshold value that needs to be exceeded for the neuron to fire.

The horizontal lines on the left, landing on the neuron body are the dendrites. The lines that end with triangles are the axons of pre-synaptic neurons that get connected to these dendrites. There are two types of triangles in the figure – those that are unfilled and those that are filled. These triangles indicate the synaptic contacts.

The filled triangles represent the inhibitory synapses and the un-filled triangles indicate the excitatory synapses. The numbers written near each triangle indicates its strength. The excitatory synaptic strengths are shown with positive numbers and the inhibitory synap-tic strengths are shown with negative numbers, so that to find their combined effect, we just need to add all of them.

And finally, the horizontal line extending to the right of the circle indicates the axon. We have ignored the leaky property of the neuron for simplicity.

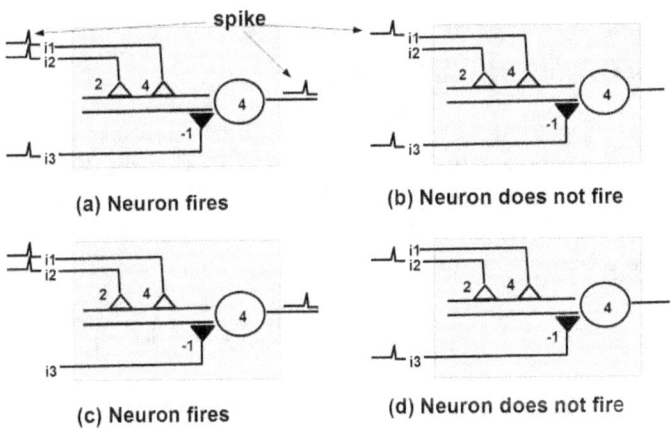

Figure 3.9: Some examples showing firing of neuron

Assume that in the Figure 3.9(a), all the pre synaptic neurons fire at the same time. What will be the combined effect of all the synapses – excitatory as well as inhibitory – in this case?

Just add all the synaptic strengths, i.e. 2+4-1 = 5. As indicated by the figure, the threshold value is just 4, which is less than the com-bined strengths of all the synapses put together. So this neuron fires since the combined input is more than the threshold.

Now let us play with this example. Assume that the pre synaptic neuron whose axon is i1 is not active (see Figure 3.9(d)). So the corresponding synapse cannot contribute anything, leaving behind just the other two inputs i2 and i3.

In this case, the combined strength of the input is 4-1=3 which is less than the threshold value of 4 and hence the neuron does not fire.

You can try other possibilities and see under what conditions the neuron fires or does not fire. Some of the possibilities are shown in Figure 3.9. In this figure the input or the output are shown as a spike.In this chapter, we saw how a simple neuron functions. The true capabilities of the neurons show up when they work as a group or when configured as a 'network' of interconnected neurons. In the next chapter, I am going to explain how these neural networks achieve various capabilities of our brain.

Before I do that, let me conclude this chapter by comparing the functioning of a neuron to the functioning of a transistor. You may skip these details, in case you are not interested in these details and go straight away to next chapter.

Neuron Vs Transistor

In the beginning of this chapter, I said that neurons are like transistors. Neurons are the basic building blocks of the brain, in the same way as transistors are basic building blocks of any computer. How do transistors work? I will not go into the detailed working of a transistor, but merely summarize its functioning.

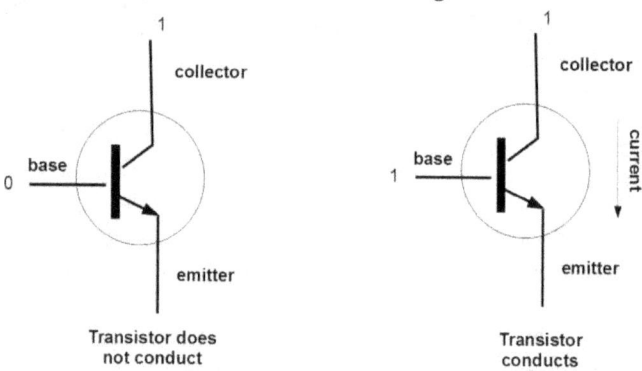

Figure 3.10: Working of a transistor

A transistor acts as a switch that allows a current to pass through it only when its 'base' is held at a 'high' voltage. If the voltage at the base is 'low', then the transistor does not allow the current to pass through it. In computer parlance a 'high' is indicated as 1 and a 'low' is indicated as 0. Figure 3.10 shows how a transistor works.

We can compare the base of a transistor to the synaptic contact that induces voltage into the neuron and the current flowing or not flowing through the transistor to the neuron firing or not firing. However, a transistor works on 'binary' inputs – 0 or 1 – whereas a neuron works on inputs that could assume various values.

Conceptually, we can visualize a transistor as a simple neuron with just one synapse of strength 1 on its dendrite and a threshold value also equal to 1, as shown in Figure 3.11

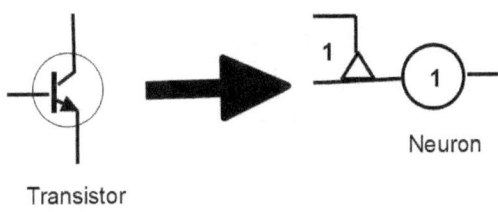

Transistor

Neuron

Figure 3.11: Transistor viewed as a simple neuron

What is interesting is to note the fact that both – neurons as well as the transistors – accomplish various functions with this apparently simple mechanism. We will see more on this in the next chapter.

4 Networks of interconnected neurons

In the previous chapter, we saw how a simple neuron functions. I explained the functioning of the neuron by comparing it to a bucket filled by dripping taps. I also compared the working of a neuron with that of a transistor that forms the basic building block of a computer.

In this chapter, I will continue on the same note and explain how a group of neurons achieves various marvelous capabilities of our brain, when they are connected as a 'network'.

Side by side, I am going to compare the working of networks of neurons with the network of transistors that also implement similar functionality in a computer. You may skip these latter details if you choose to, and focus on networks of neurons.

As I said, neurons by themselves are relatively simple devices that fire or don't fire depending on whether their input conditions meet some threshold or not. Their real capability shows up when these simple devices are interconnected in various ways. We call these interconnected neurons as networks of neurons or 'neural networks'.

Most of the capabilities of our mind – perception, decision making, memorizing, reasoning, recollecting, learning, movement of limbs, emotions, feelings, and so on – are all achieved as a result of coordinated action of neurons in various neural networks in our brain. In some way, what we refer to as 'mind' is something that 'emerges' when millions of neurons work together. Or in other words, the mind is the brain or the neurons in 'action'.

Let me now explain, one by one, how some of these functionalities are achieved by the neural networks. To simplify the discussion, I will use simple examples to highlight only the underlying principles. A detailed discussion would be taken up later in separate chapters.

Neural networks as decision makers

One of the important roles of our minds is to take decisions based on available facts. In a general case, decision making could be quite elaborate. I will take a simple example to illustrate the ability of the neural networks to implement decision making or reasoning.

Let us assume that we have a student John who is very studious and never misses a single class unless he is ill. Given a specific time of the day, we would like to know whether John is in school or not.

Figure 4.1 shows a simple neural network that can be used to infer this. There are 4 neurons – n1, n2, n3 and n4. Assume that the neuron n1 somehow finds out whether the given time falls within the school working hours and fires if it is so. Similarly, n2 fires if the given day is a holiday. And finally assume that n3 fires if John is ill. The neuron n4 is the actual decision making neuron which fires if John is at school. Assume that the threshold of n4 is 1 as shown.

Recall the conventions we used in Chapter 3. With that convention, n1 connects to n4 with a synaptic weight of 1 (excitatory synapse). Similarly, n2 and n3 are connected to n4 through inhibitory synaptic contacts of strength -1 each.

Figure 4.1: John going to school implemented as a neural network

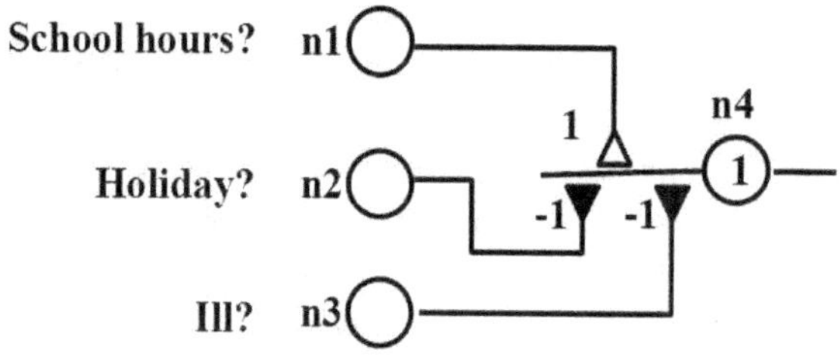

It is easy to see from the figure that n4 fires when n1 fires and neither n2 nor n3 fires (just add the synaptic weights of active axons and compare the sum with the threshold of n4).

That is, John is at school when it is school opening hours (i.e. n1 fires) and it is neither a holiday (i.e. n2 does not fire) nor John is ill (i.e. n3 does not fire). If either of n2 or n3 fire, then irrespective of the time of the day, John is not at school. So also, John is not at school if it is not school opening hours (i.e. n1 does not fire).

Let me show how same decision making can be implemented in a transistor network inside a computer. You can skip the following details if you choose to.

John going to school implemented as an electronic circuit

Instead of rigging up elaborate transistor networks to implement some decision making circuit, it is often easy to depict them using what are called 'logic gates'. A logic gate is a small network of transistors that implements an often used functionality. It is convenient to use them both from the point of implementation, as well as ease of understanding.

There are several types of logic gates. The often used ones are AND, OR and NOT gates. As their names suggest, an AND gate tests whether all its inputs are active (i.e. all 1). Similarly, OR gate tests if at least one of its inputs is active (i.e. at least one input is 1) and the NOT gate just inverts its input. That is, it gives an output 1 if its input is 0 and vice versa.

With these three types of gates, the decision making problem explained above can be implemented as shown in Figure 4.2.

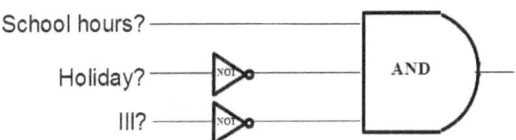

Figure 4.2: John going to school implemented using gates

As can be seen from the figure, the AND gate fires (gives an output of 1) if and only if (a) it is school hours, AND (b) it is NOT holiday, AND John is NOT ill. You can compare this circuit with the corresponding neural implementation shown in Figure 4.1.

Let me give another example. Let us say, we have a rectangle with two circles drawn inside it, as shown in Figure 4.3. These circles may be shaded or un-shaded. If we consider all combinations, there are 4 possibilities as shown in Figure 4.3.

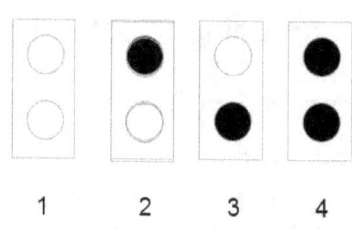

Figure 4.3: Four possible patterns

Let us say that out of these 4 combinations we are given one and want to decide whether it is a pattern with at least one shaded circle. This decision problem can

1   2   3   4

be implemented as shown in using a simple neural network. The neuron in Figure 4.4 fires if any one (or both) of the circles is shaded.

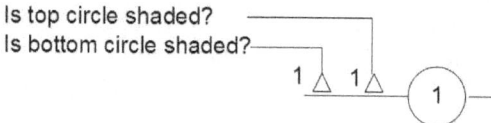

Figure 4.4 Does the pattern have at least one shaded circle?

Alternatively, we can slightly change the problem and ask "does the pattern have one and only one shaded circle?" Now the neural implementation becomes a bit tricky. It would be as shown in Figure 4.5.

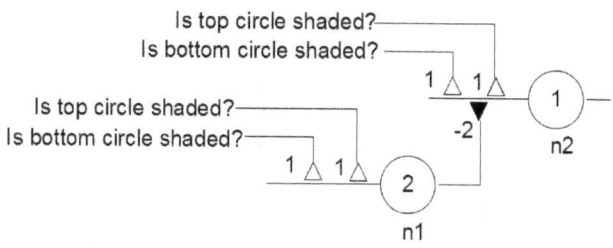

Figure 4.5: Does the pattern have one and only one shaded circle?

When the neuron n2 in Figure 4.5 fires, it means that the pattern presented has one and only one shaded circle. How does it achieve this?

If neuron n1 were not there it would have fired when either one of the circles is shaded. This is the same as the previous example. Now, the addition of neuron n1 'inhibits' it from firing when both circles are shaded. Note the inhibitor synapse with weight -2 in the figure. This is where inhibitors become important. In effect, the neuron n2 fires if and only if one and only one of the circles are shaded. And that is what we are looking for.

We can even have a single network to implement both the above decision problems. An additional control can be added to choose the decision problem we are interested in. I have shown this in Figure 4.6 , where the neuron nc is the controlling neuron.

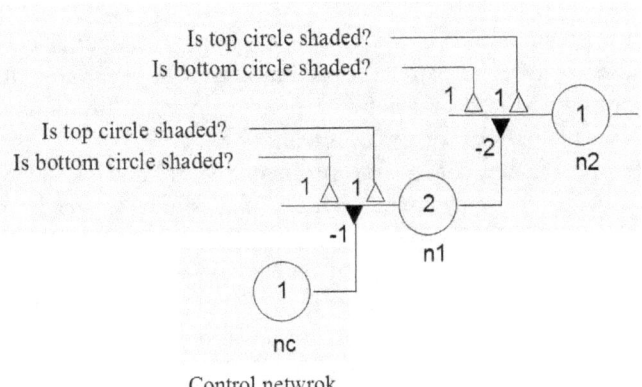

Control netwrok

Figure 4.6: Decision problem example with control

When nc fires, this network behaves like Figure 4.4, and when nc does not fire it behaves like Figure 4.5. This way of some network influencing the outcome of some other network is often useful as we will see in later chapters.

Now, there are a couple of things to note. The neural networks shown in Figure 4.4 and Figure 4.5 are not unique. The same problems could have been solved using several (in fact, infinitely many) different neural networks.

Each of these networks may employ different number of neurons connected in variety of ways; but they all could perform the same decision making. Even the synaptic strengths as well as the thresholds are not unique either. In Figure 4.5 you can replace input synaptic strengths of the neuron n1 by 0.5 instead of 1 and change the threshold to 1. That would not alter the functioning of this network in anyway.

Try playing with synaptic strengths, thresholds in the above examples and convince yourselves. You can also try cooking up different networks that achieve the same functionality as the above two networks. You may wonder whether there is a minimum number of neurons needed to implement a given functionality. That is a difficult question. Think about it!

Neural networks for pattern recognition

In the previous section, we saw how neural networks can decide whether a particular pattern is presented to it or not. Some neuron at the output of the neural network fires or does not fire depending on whether the pattern was present or not.

Supposing we change the problem slightly and would want the network to recognize what pattern was shown instead of saying whether a particular pattern was shown.

What exactly do we mean by recognizing? Consider our day-today activity of recognizing various things. When an animal with 4 legs, a tail, probably horns, and so on appear before us we recognize it as a cow. If it is a short animal with a wagging tail, we recognize it as a dog.

Basically, we are associating the appearance of an object with a word and a mental meaning. In general, recognition is an act of associating an image with a mental 'code' assigned to that image. To make it more general, the image need not be a visual image. It could be a fragrance, or taste, or sound, or a touch sensation. In all these cases, recognition involves just that – associating what is perceived to some internal mental code.

Let me take a simple example of visual recognition. Take for example, the 4 patterns shown in Figure 4.3. Let us say that when we recognize a particular pattern among the 4 possible patterns, we make a hand gesture, say, raise the forefinger if pattern 1 is recognized, the middle finger if pattern 2 is shown, the index finger if pattern 3 is shown and the small finger if pattern 4 is shown.

Our fingers are controlled by signals from the brain. One or more muscles around the finger joints have to contract for the finger to rise. These contractions are achieved by sending signals through the axons of the neurons connected to these muscles. The muscle contracts when a particular neuron that is connected to the muscle fires.

This allows the finger to stretch.

For the sake of our discussion, let us make a simple case where each of our fingers is controlled by a single neuron and the finger rises whenever this neuron fires. To implement our example recognition problem we need 4 such neurons each controlling one finger. Since the pattern has two distinctly shaded circles, we need four inputs, each of which tells us which of the circles is shaded or not shaded.

How do we realize this recognition problem with 4 inputs (corresponding to status of two circles) and 4 outputs (corresponding to 4 fingers), in terms of a simple neural network? Figure 4.7 shows one such possibility.

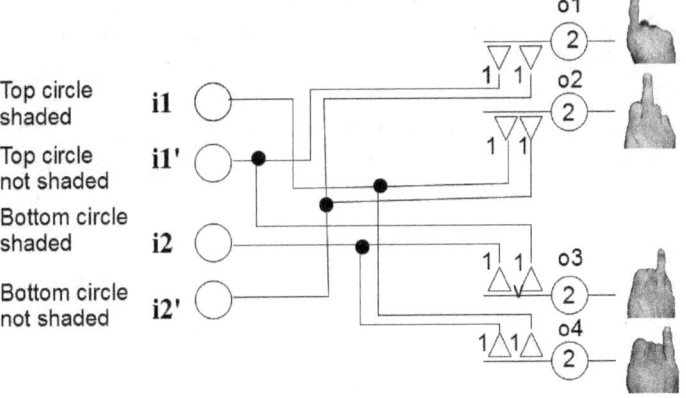

Figure 4.7: A simple pattern recognition example

In this figure, I have assumed that i1 and i2 fire whenever top or bottom circles are shaded, i1' and i2' fire whenever respective circles are not shaded. o1 through o4 are 4 output neurons each controlling one finger as I have discussed earlier. Trace this network, following each input combination, and convince yourselves that this network indeed does the recognition job as we defined.

A recognition problem is not always as simple as that discussed above. In general, there are many issues that need to be considered before a pattern is recognized. I will discuss those details in a later chapter. For the time being, let us slightly generalize the above problem.

A simple character recognition neural network

Instead of recognizing simple arbitrary patterns as in the previous example, let us say that we want to recognize characters from English alphabet. We routinely do this recognition when we read something. But how does our mind perform this?

In the simplest case, we break a letter into columns of dots one below the other as shown in Figure 4.8. In this figure, we have assumed that a character is broken into 5 columns; each with 7 circles stacked one above the other. All together there are 7 X 5 = 35 circles in this grid. These circles can be shaded or not shaded to represent some character in the English alphabet. The Figure 4.8 shows letter 'A'.

In the light of the previous example, we can assume that each column is a pattern to be recognized. The shaded circles in the previous example are the dots in the present case and the un-shaded circles, the absence of dots.

Figure 4.8: Simple character recognition network

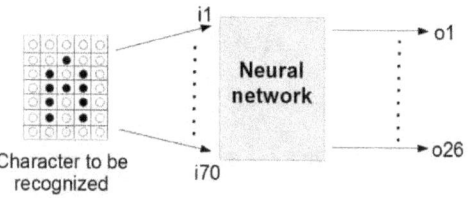

I don't wish to give the elaborate design of this neural network, but indicate it by a rectangular box as shown in Figure 4.8.

As in the previous case, this neural network can have 70 inputs – i1 through i70 - and 26 outputs - o1 through o26. 70 inputs because there are 35 circles in this case, each of which can be shaded or unshaded.

Assuming that we are interested only in recognizing 26 letters of English alphabet and adopt a 'position code' as in the previous example; we need this network to have 26 outputs. If the first output is active (i.e. the corresponding neuron fires) then it is the first letter in the alphabet, and so on. The position of the active output indicates the position of the alphabet in the alphabet list. Let me repeat, this arrangement is just one of the possibilities.

How does this neural network look like? Definitely it would have many more neurons than the earlier case and connected in more complex fashion. In the previous example, I used my knowledge about the design of 'decoders' in digital circuits to arrive at the network. The previous example is a typical 2 to 4 digital decoder.

A 2 to 4 decoder implementation (you may skip this)

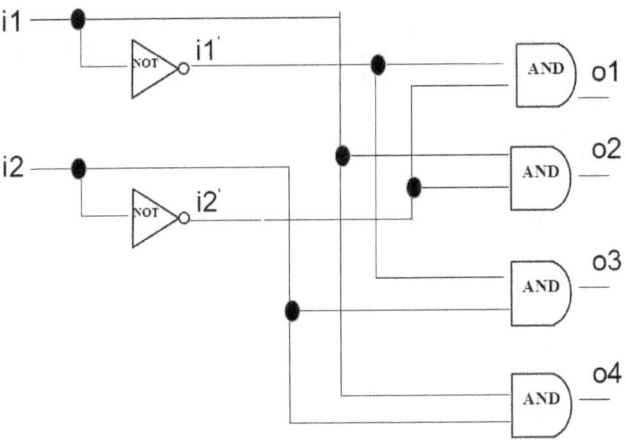

Figure 4.9: A 2 to 4 decoder

But neural networks are not formed using digital design rules. They are formed by more biologically driven processes that I will be discussing in Chapter 5 . Let us not worry about those issues right now. Let us focus on what this network can do.

This network recognizes the input character and outputs a 'position code' corresponding to the recognized letter. But there is a catch here. In the previous simple pattern example, there were just 2 circles that could be shaded or not shaded. That is why there are 2 X 2 = 4 possible patterns. But in the present case however, there are 7 X 5 = 35 circles each of which can be shaded or not shaded. So, there are 2 X 2 .....X 2 (35 times) possible patterns. You know how big this number is? It is greater than 1 followed by 30 zeroes!

Among that huge number of patterns, the number of patterns that are of interest to us are only 26. What would happen if some pattern that is not any of the 26 letters is presented to the neural network of ours? The simplest possibility is that it would say that the pattern is unrecognizable. But normally, neural networks do something smarter. They guess the closest pattern that corresponds to one of the 26 letters.

For example, all the four patterns shown in Figure 4.10 may be recognized as letter 'A' even though they are not identical to letter 'A'.

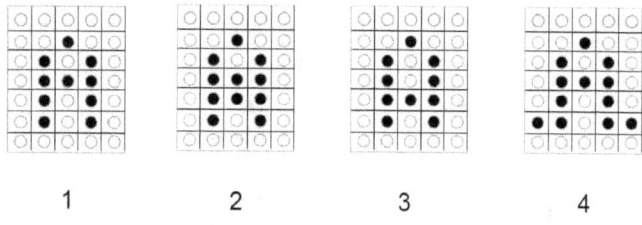

1   2   3   4

Figure 4.10: All the four patterns may be recognized as 'A'

In other words, neural networks can 'approximate' the input patterns to the 'nearest' possible pattern and produce a useful and probably correct output.

For most humans it is trivial to recognize hand written letters where each letter can vary substantially from the standard printed form of the letter. With all the sophistication of computer programs, such a feat is almost impossible for a computer. This is just one area where we – the possessors of neural networks - are better than computers.

Neural networks as pattern completers

In the last section, I talked about how neural networks can do pattern recognition. I also explained how neural networks can guess a pattern even when the input has minor deviations as compared to the real pattern. In other words, the neural networks are immune to minor variations in the input patterns.

When neural networks are used to recognize complex patterns, more interesting things happen. A complex pattern may have several 'features' and may need several neural networks to identify each of these features. Each of these networks work in parallel analyzing different features of a single pattern. Once these features are individually recognized, there could be yet another neural network that could pool all the information from each of the networks and come to an overall conclusion about the pattern being recognized.

Let me explain with an example. Consider a cow being recognized by a set of neural networks as shown in Figure 4.11. A cow has several features - it has horns, it has an udder, it has the typical bovine neck, and so on.

Let us assume that Networks 1 to 3 recognize each of these features independently. Let us also assume that output of these networks is fed to another network namely Network 4 which finally takes a decision that the animal being recognized is a cow.

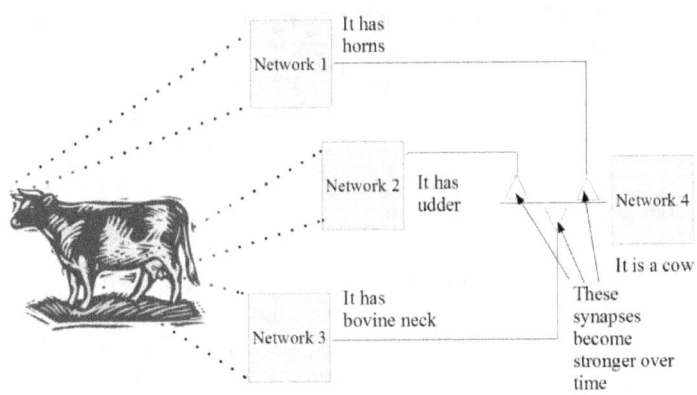

Figure 4.11: Pattern completion example

In the figure, I have shown the feeding of outputs of these networks to Network 4 by means of individual excitatory synaptic contacts. To start with, Network 4 recognizes the cow only when all the 3 inputs are active. But what happens when the cow is repeatedly presented to these networks?

For reasons that I will be explaining in Chapter 5, gradually, the 3 synapses shown in Figure 4.11 grow in strength every time the cow is presented and a stage will be reached when each of them can excite Network 4 on its own.

When that happens, Network 4 recognizes the cow even when

only some features are presented. That is, after some exposures to the cow and proper strengthening of synapses, just by looking at the horns or the udder or the neck, the Network 4 can recognize the animal as cow!

This capability of the neural networks is called the ability to 'complete the pattern'. That is the ability to recognize a complex pattern even when only a partial pattern is presented. The neural network appears to 'fill in the blanks'. This is yet another capability that makes us – the owners of neural networks - superior to computers.

Neural networks as universal mappers

Before I explain what a universal mapper is, let us briefly recollect the neural networks we looked at in the previous sections. In the simple pattern recognition example (refer to Figure 4.7), the neural network we used responded with 4 outputs. The position of the active (i.e. the corresponding neuron firing) output among the 4 outputs indicated what was recognized.

This network had 4 inputs. In other words, this network associated particular 'value' of these 4 inputs to particular 'value' of the 4 outputs. Or it mapped a 4 input to a 4 output.

Instead of raising one of the four fingers as shown in this example, we could have signaled the same thing using just two fingers, say forefinger and middle finger. When pattern 1 is recognized, neither of the fingers is raised; when pattern 2 is recognized, just the forefinger; when pattern 3 is recognized, just the middle finger; and finally when the pattern 4 is recognized, both fingers are raised. This would have served the same purpose of recognition. We could have had a neural network to output such an 'encoded' output.

Similarly, in the case of the character recognition example we discussed in Figure 4.8, the neural network we used mapped 35 inputs to 26 outputs. Alternatively, we could have had a neural network that mapped these 35 inputs to just 8 outputs and still perform the same function. This is what a computer typically does.

When a computer recognizes a character, it maps the character to an '8 bit code' called ASCII code corresponding to the character. For example, the letter 'A' shown in Figure 4.8 would have been mapped to the 8 bit code '01000001' (or a hexadecimal number 0x41).

In general, we can have neural networks to map any set of inputs to any other set of outputs. That is why they are called 'universal mappers'. This capability of the neural networks comes handy in realizing several functionalities of the brain.

Neural networks as memories

What is a memory? Memory is just some record of event that has happened earlier in time. All of us have some capability to memorize things. We have different types of memories. Our short term memories remember the events that happened just a while ago or may be a few days ago. But after sometime we tend to forget them.

There are other memories, for example long term memories that last for months or even lifelong. Many of us clearly remember the interesting events that happened to us during our childhood days. We rarely forget them and enjoy recollecting them. The 'lifetime' of such memories are normally very long or probably they last forever.

There are other memories which we call associative memories. When you look at the following picture of an Indian folk drummer, instantly you may recollect several events that had happened long back, when you had visited India last time.

Figure 4.12: An Indian folk artist playing the drum

You 'associate' those events to the picture you are seeing now. Similarly, the fragrance of some flower may remind you of someone who loved those flowers. These memories associate one event with a chain of events that occurred in the past. If you remember one of these events, whole chain of events would flash in one go.

There are other memories, for example procedural memories. If you are a good cook, you not only remember the entire list of ingredients to be added to a particular recipe but also the entire step by step procedure of making that recipe.

If you are a cricket player, your hands 'know' how to hit the ball in a particular situation. In other words, the hand movements needed in a specific context are 'remembered' by your brain, though you may not be explicitly aware of the same.

All these are different kinds of memories. And there can be many more. How each of these memories is implemented by our brain is quite a complex process. I will be discussing some of these in greater detail in chapters that follow. At the moment, I will explain some simple underlying mechanisms that enable these memories to be realized by the brain.

All these memories are realized by various types of neural networks. The most basic idea behind how neural networks remember things is the following.

A simple neural memory

Consider the simple neural network shown in Figure 4.13. Look at the cross connected neurons n2 and n3. The axon of n2 is connected to the dendrite of n3 and the axon of n3 is connected back to the dendrite of n2 through the synaptic contacts as shown. Further, the neuron n1 is connected to neuron n2.

Figure 4.13 A simple memory implementation

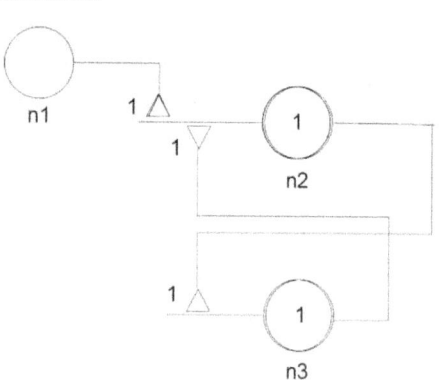

Now, what will happen when n1 fires? When n1 fires, irrespective of what is going on in n3, n2 fires because of the choice of synaptic strengths and the threshold of n2. When this happens, since the axon of n2 is connected back to the dendrite of n3, synaptic strength and threshold of n3 being appropriate, n3 also fires.

Let us now consider the case that n1 stops firing. But n2 would continue to fire since one of its inputs coming from n3 triggers it to fire. The process continues and both n2 and n3 fire perpetually, irrespective of whether n1 is still firing. That means n2 and n3 'remember' that n1 had fired once and they continue to fire to indicate that one time event. Or in other words, this cross connected network of n2 and n3 is a simple memory that would record the event of n1 firing once.

These kind of neural networks are called re-entrant networks, since the output of one neuron re-enters itself through another neuron

As I said earlier, there are various types of memories. The most interesting and probably the most useful among them are the associative memories. Let us see the basic principle governing these associative memories.

Simple associative memories

As I said earlier, associative memories associate some event with some other event or a chain of events. Let me explain the basic principle behind these memories by means of a simple example.

You probably have never heard of the word 'Durian". Actually it is a rare South Asian fruit which is considered to be the king of fruits by those who love it.

Before you read the word "Durian" above, your memory had no record of such a word. Suppose I show you a picture of Durian, that picture gets recorded in your memory. Not only that this memory record automatically gets "associated" with the word "Durian", also recorded in your brain.

From now on, when you hear the word "Durian", immediately the picture of the fruit appears in your mind. Or when you ever see this fruit, your mind automatically tells you that it is Durian. How does this happen?

Refer Figure 4.14(a). I have shown a highly simplified figure of how this happens. When you first hear or read the word 'Durian' it gets recorded in your verbal memory as shown in the figure. Next time, when you again hear or read the same word, the word gets identified since it is already stored in memory.

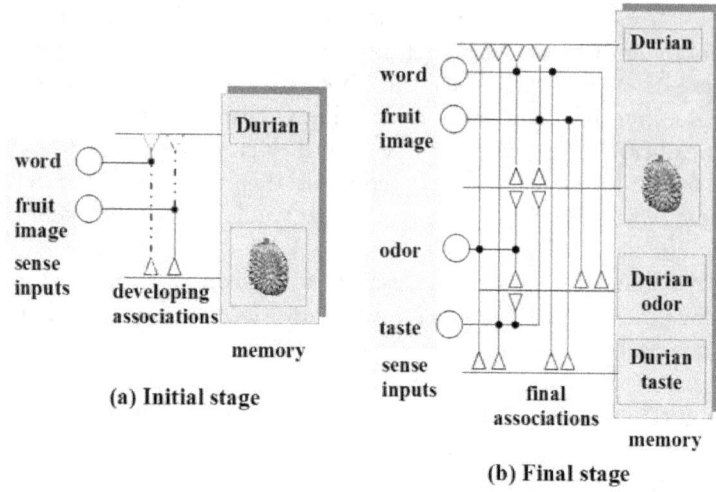

Figure 4.14: Associative memory example

In Figure 4.14(a), I have simply shown this fact by showing a neuron that excites the memory corresponding to the word Durian through the synaptic connection (shown as solid line) as shown. The strength of this connection is sufficient to fire the neurons in the memory corresponding to the word.

Next you see the actual fruit or an image of the fruit. Once again a corresponding record is made in the memory as shown in the figure, and corresponding synaptic contacts (shown as solid line) are also established for future retrieval. At this stage, word memory can be retrieved by hearing the word Durian and the picture memory by seeing the image or the fruit. What will happen when someone shows you the fruit and also tells you that it is Durian?

This is what I have tried to show using dotted lines in Figure 4.14(a). The dotted lines indicate the gradual setting up of synaptic connections to record the fact that the word 'Durian' and the fruit image are associated. Repeated exposure to the fruit and its name, happening together, would strengthen this synaptic connection.

Once this connection becomes sufficiently strong, you can retrieve the word 'Durian' as well as the stored image of Durian, either when you hear the word Durian or when you see the actual fruit or its image.

What you have done is that you have built an 'associative memory' associating the word 'Durian' with the corresponding image of the fruit. Now on, no one needs to show you the fruit and say that it is Durian since you have already built the association between the two. I will come to the details of how these associations are built, in Chapter 5.

As you get more and more familiar with the fruit, you build further associations. You associate its supposedly offensive odor with whatever you know about it already. Once you taste the fruit, you also record its supposedly fantastic taste and associate the same with the word, image and odor recorded earlier. I have indicated this in Figure 4.14(b).

From now on, mere mention of the word 'durian' is sufficient to recall its image, odor as well as the taste. You may also record your subjective judgment – 'excellent fruit' or 'hopelessly repelling fruit' – and associate that judgment also with your other memories of Durian. This way, the memory of durian goes on building up.

As you might have noticed, single information stored in memory can be recalled in several ways. Also, recalling one bit of information simultaneously retrieves all the associated information with no extra effort and almost in parallel. This is in contrast to the memories used in a computer which is generally not associative.

Computer memory (you may skip this section)

Normal computer memories are what are called 'random access memories (RAM)'. To access something stored in such a memory, you need something called an 'address' corresponding to that stored information. When and only when this address is presented to the memory, that information and only that information would be available. You cannot retrieve that information using any other address.

But there are special purpose computer memories that can work like the associative memory our brain has. These memories are called 'content addressed memories (CAM)'. These memories though, are much restricted in their functionality and generally are expensive to build. Unlike a RAM, a CAM uses some pre-assigned code - 'key' - to access information stored in it. These codes can be arbitrary and need not be a sequence of numbers as in the case of RAM addresses. CAMs 'associate' the 'keys' with whatever is stored.

On the other extreme, there are rarely used associative memories such as 'set associative caches' or 'translation look aside buffers

(TLBs)' that allow a 'range' of addresses to access a memory location. But none of these match anywhere the capabilities of our brain!

I would be talking more on memories and associations in later chapters. In the next section, let us see some interesting things that happen because of the dynamic firing of the neurons in a neural network.

Dynamics of neural networks

In all the examples we discussed in the previous sections, we talked as if the pre-synaptic neurons fire all at once. To simplify our discussions we also assumed that a neuron can be excited by just one spike from a pre-synaptic neuron. In reality it is not so.

Neurons fire continuously at different rates and just one input spike cannot make another neuron fire. Often thousands of neurons get connected to a single neuron and they may fire at different order and at different rates. What happens in such a dynamic scenario?

Let us first consider the dynamics of a post-synaptic neuron connected to a firing pre-synaptic neuron (not shown) as shown in Figure 4.15.

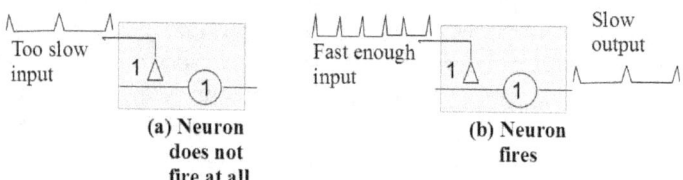

(a) Neuron does not fire at all

(b) Neuron fires

Figure 4.15: Network dynamics example 1

Consider the case (a) when the pre-synaptic neuron fires rather slowly. Recall the bucket analogy I gave earlier in Chapter 3.

A leaky bucket kept under a dripping tap can get filled only if the falling water drops are fast enough to compensate for the leakage in the bucket. Otherwise, whatever water that gets added to the bucket from the dripping taps gets drained by the leakage.

Similarly, if the input spikes of a neuron are too slow, the neuron may never reach its firing level due to the inherent leakage. This is what is shown in Figure 4.15(a).

The situation changes when the input becomes fast enough to build the charge inside the neuron, in spite of the leakage. In that case the neuron starts to fire. This firing may be at a slower rate. But the neuron does fire as shown in Figure 4.15(b). What it means is that, it is not sufficient for the input neuron to fire, but it should fire at a minimum rate to excite the post-synaptic neuron.

If we now consider the scenario when two or more pre-synaptic neurons try to excite the post-synaptic neuron as shown in Figure 4.16, we see more interesting things.

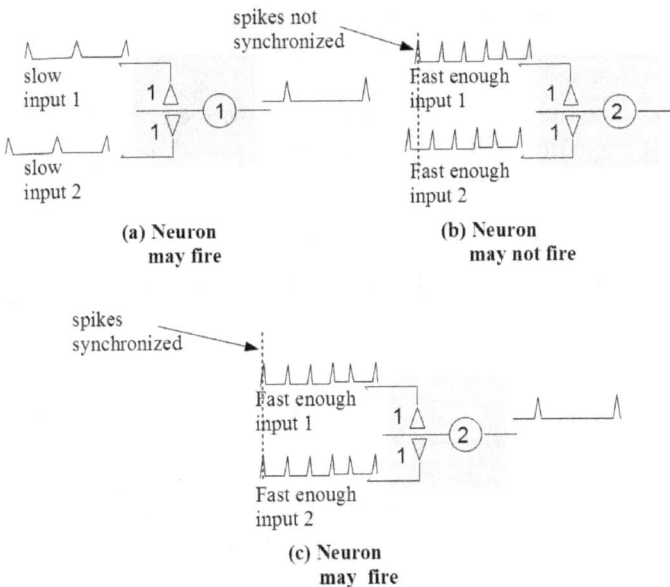

Figure 4.16: Network dynamics example 2

In Figure 4.16(a) I have shown a neuron with two inputs each of which is relatively slow. But this neuron may still fire as shown, since the two inputs get added up and compensate for the leakage in the neuron.

In Figure 4.16(b) I have slightly modified the case by changing the threshold of the neuron to 2 instead of 1. Now the neuron may not fire even if the inputs are quite fast. This happens if the input spikes don't occur at the same time, or they are not 'synchronized' as in this case.

The spikes from the pre-synaptic neurons occur at different times and they may not really get added up sufficiently to compensate for the loss due to leakage.

However, if we ensure that these two input spike trains are synchronized as shown in Figure 4.16(c) the neuron may fire. Now the spikes get added up and may compensate for the loss due to leakage. There are several other possible scenarios. You can cook up your own examples and see how neural networks behave under different conditions.

The conclusion one can draw from the above examples is that the behavior of the same neural network depends not only on the synaptic strengths and the thresholds, but also on the 'spiking rate' as well as the 'spiking order' of the pre-synaptic neurons.

Whole lot of interesting things can happen due to this neural dynamics. In the next section we will see how the brain utilizes some of these properties of the neural networks to its advantage.

Interesting applications of neural dynamics

In this section, I consider networks of neurons and show how they interact with each other and what its consequences are. Take for example, the two networks shown in Figure 4.17(a). For the sake of simplicity, I have shown Network 1 as containing only one neuron. This is just to illustrate the basic idea.

Left to itself, Network 1 would have fired, probably at a slower rate, in response to the input spike train. Now consider what the other network does to it. Network 2 occasionally tries to stimulate Network 1, so that Network 1 keeps firing at a better rate than before. In other words, Network 2 boosts the working of Network 1.

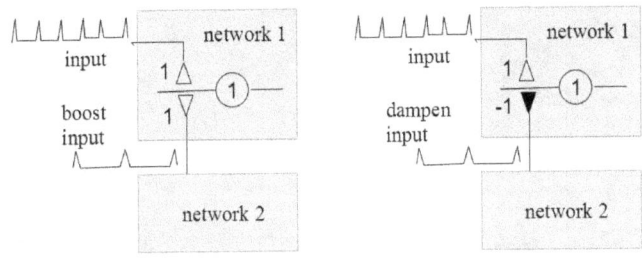

(a) network 2 tries to boost the firing of network 1

(b) network 2 tries to dampen the firing of network 1

Figure 4.17: Network dynamics application

In the previous case Network 2 uses an excitatory synaptic input to boost Network 1. Now consider Figure 4.17(b).

Here, Network 2 uses a inhibitory output to occasionally prevent Network 1 from firing. In other words, in this case Network 2 dampens Network 1. These kinds of boosting and dampening have several applications.

Often there are one or more neural networks, each producing a possible solution to a problem in a given situation. These networks compete among themselves and the winner succeeds in influencing the final outcome. The losers gradually get dampened out and would have no effect on the outcome.

Alternatively, they may form coalitions of neural networks, with the members of a coalition supporting each other and opposing the members of other coalitions. In all these cases, the boosting and dampening mechanisms I described above come handy.

In this chapter we assumed some neural networks without saying how such networks are formed in our brain. This is one of the most important issues and not yet fully understood. In the next chapter I will discuss some of the ways in which different neural networks may get formed in our brain.

5 How are neural networks formed?

In the previous chapter we saw how different networks of neurons implement various capabilities of our brain. In the examples we saw, we assumed some interconnection between different neurons. We also assumed some synaptic strength and the threshold values. You probably wonder who sets up these neural networks and when! In this chapter, I am going to explain to you how various neural networks get formed in our brain.

Before I get into these technicalities, as usual let me start with a mundane example. Let us say, you want to construct a house for yourself. Where do you start from? You probably consult an architect who prepares a 'blue print' for you. This blue print has the overall detail of the house you want to get constructed. How many rooms it should have, how these rooms are organized, how many doors and windows, what kind of roof, and so on. That is, a blue print is a broad outline of your house which is yet to be constructed.

Next you give this blue print to a mason and ask him to build the house. Mason takes the blue print as the starting point. Based on the guidelines provided in the blueprint, the mason starts building the foundation, lays each brick and so on. While doing that, the mason does not go by the blueprint since the blueprint does not give that level of detail. The mason decides things based on the 'ground realities' – size and shape of each brick, minor modifications that may need to be made to put the structure together.

Simultaneously, he may consult you at various stages and make alterations depending on your inputs. So, not everything is done as per the blueprint. For one thing, blueprint cannot possibly have all the minute details, nor the architect who drew the blueprint could foresee all the dynamic events that could happen during the process of construction. The blueprint only provides a starting point.

Finally, you have completed the construction. Now it is time to tidy up things. During construction lot of additional structures could have been built to aide in the construction such as scaffolding, supports and so on. Now it is time to dismantle all that extra stuff that has served its purpose.

Now that your house is ready, you probably would start living in that newly constructed house. Over a period of time, you may make several alterations in the house to suite your needs or depending on the circumstances.

You probably have a new member in your family and so you may add an extra room to your house. Or probably you would like to give a new look to your house by making some minor changes. All these details were not in the initial blueprint, nor were they anticipated by the mason while constructing the house. These are dynamic changes that happen over a period of time.

After several years, you may come to a stage when your house may show signs of aging. The roof may start leaking. You may have to re-lay the roof or reinforce it in some other way. You may also have to replace some window sill that may have got worn off and so on. So, your changes now are mainly related to maintenance of an old house.

The formation of the neural networks in our brain also follows a very similar pattern. Let us now see how this happens.

The basic networks are formed as guided by the genetic blueprint

The blueprint for the initial setting up of the neural networks in our brain is in our genes. We inherit our genes from our parents. The broad outline of the wiring of our brain was in these genes. Probably with some changes, we pass on these blueprints to our children.

As I said earlier, a blueprint does not have all the minute details. The process of wiring of the brain, though guided by the genetic blueprint, also gets influenced by the prevailing conditions that exist at the time of formation of the brain. Let us see how all these things happen.

Three weeks after conception

In around 3 weeks after the formation of an embryo, cells divide, producing more new cells. These cells transform the embryo into a long narrow tube like structure as shown in Figure 5.1. At one end of the tube, three bulges get formed. These bulges are the brain in the early stages of formation.

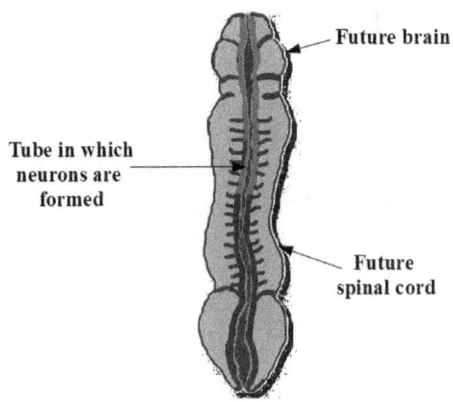

Figure 5.1: Early development of the brain

The narrow tube is the future spinal cord. Some of the newly formed cells grow into different organs. Others formed inside the narrow tube become neurons. Which cell has to become an organ and which one has to become a neuron is largely pre-decided by 'the blue print' in the genes as well as the environment in which they are formed.

The neurons are the 'bricks' that would later be used to form the networks in the brain which is yet to develop.

4 to 7 weeks after conception

In roughly 4 week's time, the three bulges shown in Figure 5.1 grow into roughly the shape of a primitive brain. The neurons that are formed in the narrow tube start migrating into this primitive brain to take their proper places.

Axons start developing from these neurons. These axons start getting longer and longer in search of their destinations. Their destinations are the dendrites that are also formed on other neurons at the same time. At the point where the axons meet the dendrites, synaptic contacts get formed. Further, various chemical changes decide the kind of neurotransmitters produced by each of the synapses and the way the dendrite junctions respond to these neurotransmitters.

Once these neurons reach their respective destinations and the axon/dendrites get developed, these neurons interconnect among themselves into complex networks that will perform various functions of the brain. Here again, the genetic blueprint comes into play.

After 3 months

The growth of the brain continues and it resembles more like the final form. But it still lacks the folds that are seen in the adult brain. Continuous changes in the neural connections take place to refine the structure of the neural networks formed earlier.

Beyond 6 months

The changes in the brain continue. Folds on the surface of the brain start appearing. The shape of the brain almost resembles its final form. The neural connections continuously get refined.

Several unnecessary connections get removed. As many as half the neurons die owing to 'apoptosis' - pre-programmed cell deaths - by the time the child grows into an adult. The neural connections that remain make the brain more efficient and powerful.

This is how the initial neural networks are formed in the brain. These networks perform various predefined functions of the brain and are more or less fixed during the life time of the person. These networks are like the pre-connected functional units of a computer.

Pre-connected functional units of a computer (you can skip this)

The CPU (Central Processing Unit) of a computer has several pre-connected functional units, each performing a specific function. There is at least one ALU (Arithmetic and Logical Unit), an FPU

(Floating Point Unit), cache controller, graphics processor, I/O controller (Input/ Output controller) and so on. All these pre-connected networks of transistors are formed when the CPU was fabricated.

Once fabricated, these don't change and remain throughout the lifetime of the CPU performing respective functions. These are optimally designed and highly efficient in performing the respective tasks.

Coming back to the pre-connected neural networks in the brain, just these networks are not sufficient to handle various situations that a person encounters during his life time. New neural networks have to be formed as and when the need arises.

Most networks are formed as a result of interaction with the world

Various new networks are formed during the life time of an individual as he interacts with the world around. Some of these networks could be transient and some may last forever.

There are networks formed to store information in memory, to store sequences of limb movements, or as temporary holders for sense inputs, or as record of experiences and feelings, and so on.

How are these networks formed? We will see the formation of some such neural networks in the chapters that follow. For now, let me discuss some of the basic mechanisms that govern the formation of these networks.

As I discussed in the previous section, many of the neurons that were in the brain during the formation of the brain got connected among themselves into specific neural networks guided by the genetic blueprint and the prevailing conditions at that time.

What happens to rest of the neurons? If we see the brain, layers of such 'spare' neurons are distributed all along the periphery of the brain, pre-connected in a specific way. These 'spare' neurons form specific networks as and when the person starts interacting with the world after birth.

How exactly these spare neurons are pre-connected is not fully understood. Let us assume that they are connected in a random way.

But their interconnections are not strong enough to make them perform any specific functions. They are like reserve stores that can be used for achieving future functionality.

As we have already seen in Chapter 4, one or more structurally dissimilar neural networks can exhibit the same functionality. Each of these neural networks can have different number of neurons and they may be connected in different ways. But still all of these can potentially perform the same operation.

So, what is important is the strength of the synaptic connections between the neurons. By appropriately varying these strengths, we can make the same network perform different operations. The reason why I am stressing this point is to drive home the point that the initial connection of these 'spare' neurons is immaterial. It is the synaptic strengths that matters.

Now the main question is how are these synaptic strengths modified later? There is no central entity in the brain that sits and decides the strengths of connections in each newly formed neural network. The brain does not function that way. For most purposes, unlike a computer, the brain is a completely distributed processing system. That being the case, how does the brain alter the synaptic strengths?

How does a computer do it? (You can skip these details if you wish)

Analogues of neural networks that are implemented in a computer – the so called 'artificial neural networks', use what are called 'back propagation algorithms' to iteratively change the synaptic strengths. These mathematically intensive computations compare the output of the neural network in the formation, with the expected output, and some function of the 'error' is used to make a change in the synaptic strengths as a corrective measure.

In a series of steps, the synaptic strengths are altered and finally the errors settle to well within acceptable limits. When that happens, the synaptic strengths are frozen. The point to note is that the computation of errors, feeding them back, and so on, is done in a centralized and sequential manner.

In the next section let is see how the brain does it.

Activity based synaptic plasticity

How does the brain achieve the variations in synaptic strengths depending on the need? This had been a mystery till a Canadian psychologist Donald Hebb made the following speculation, way back in 1949. Though Hebb had no way of verifying his speculation but later he was widely accepted to be right. His speculation was what we now commonly term as the Hebbian rule. His original speculation was the following.

> *"When an axon of a cell (neuron) 'A' is near enough to excite cell(neuron) 'B' or repeatedly or persistently takes part in firing it, some growth or metabolic change takes place in both the cells such that 'A''s efficiency, as one of the cells firing 'B', is increased".*

Before I explain what this implies, let me remind you that most neurons in the brain are connected to hundreds or probably thousands of other neurons. Also, a single neuron cannot by itself succeed in firing another neuron to which it is connected through its synaptic contact. It is the collective action of more than one neuron that often succeeds in firing a post synaptic neuron.

In such a scenario, what the above speculation says is that when some neuron on its own gets almost close to firing another neuron or succeeds in firing it in collaboration with other neurons, and if that happens repeatedly, then some changes happen in both the pre and post synaptic neurons, such that pre synaptic neuron becomes more capable of firing the post synaptic neuron in the next such occasion. Let me explain with some examples.

In Figure 5.2(a) I have shown a neuron that is connected to a pre-synaptic neuron through a synaptic contact of strength 1. Since this synaptic strength is less than the threshold 2 of the post-synaptic neuron, the pre-synaptic neuron fails to excite it to firing.

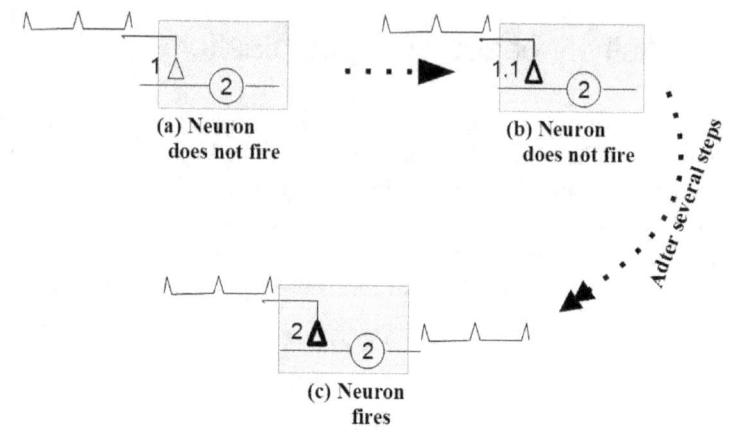

Figure 5.2: Hebbian rule example 1

But after some attempts to excite the neuron, the synaptic strength gradually increases to 1.1 as shown in Figure 5.2(b). But still the pre-synaptic neuron is unable to excite the neuron since the strength is still way below what is needed.

After several attempts, the synaptic strength gradually grows to 2 and the pre-synaptic neuron succeeds in firing the post-synaptic neuron as shown in Figure 5.2(c).

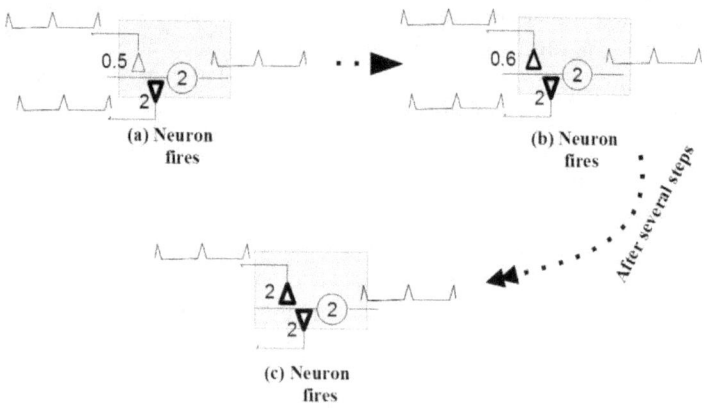

Figure 5.3: Hebbian rule example 2

Let me take another example. In this case, the post-synaptic neuron is connected to more than one pre-synaptic neuron as shown in

Figure 5.3(a). Here, there are two pre-synaptic neurons each trying to excite the post-synaptic neuron.

The top synaptic contact has a weight 0.5 which is too inadequate to excite the post-synaptic neuron on its own. However, the other pre-synaptic neuron with the synaptic strength of 2 (the bottom one) is quite capable of exciting the post-synaptic neuron.

Let us see what happens when both these neurons try to fire the post-synaptic neuron together. Even though the strength of upper synapse is not sufficient to excite the neuron, as per the Hebbian rule this strength gradually rises to 0.6 and so on as shown in Figure 5.3(b). This will continue if it so happens that both these pre-synaptic neurons fire together or within a time window.

After several steps of firing together, the strength of the upper neuron rises to the required value of 2. Once this happens, this neuron can excite the post-synaptic neuron on its own without the help of the other neuron as shown in Figure 5.3(c).

There are other ways these synaptic changes can happen. It is possible for a pre-synaptic neuron to develop additional synaptic contacts with the post-synaptic neuron so that the combined strength of all its synapses meets the required threshold of the post-synaptic neuron. All these cases are examples of 'synaptic plasticity' where a synapse adopts itself to the situation.

The brain also has mechanisms to do just the opposite of synaptic strengthening. A synapse gets weaker gradually unless it is periodically coaxed to grow in strength. So there is a balance between the strengthening of a synapse and its weakening.

How does activity driven synaptic plasticity work? Scientists are working on various ways this could be happening.

Some possible mechanisms of activity based synaptic plasticity

As we discussed in Chapter 3, a synaptic contact succeeds in exciting a neuron to which it is connected, by releasing chemical messengers called neuro-transmitters. These neuro-transmitters finally succeed in making the post synaptic neuron fire. Some scientists are working on the possibility of similar chemical messengers fed back from an excited neuron to all the synapses connecting to it. These messengers can coax these synapses to grow in strength. This is called 'back firing'.

Some scientists are working on the possibility of 'gene expression' mechanisms. Certain genes that are normally not active get activated under certain conditions and when they get activated they induce formation of new synaptic connections between neurons.

There could be other mechanisms as well.

Reward based synaptic plasticity

It is commonly observed that animals can be trained to perform various physical actions by inducing them with rewards. In one typical experiment conducted by the scientists, a cat was put into a box closed by a gate. There were a couple of levers on the gate of the box pressing which the cat could escape from the box.

If the cat escapes the box by pressing the levers, it was rewarded with some food and was put back into the box. But the food was given only if the lever was pressed after a bell sound is made. If there was no preceding bell sound, the cat would get no reward even if it pressed the lever and escaped from the box.

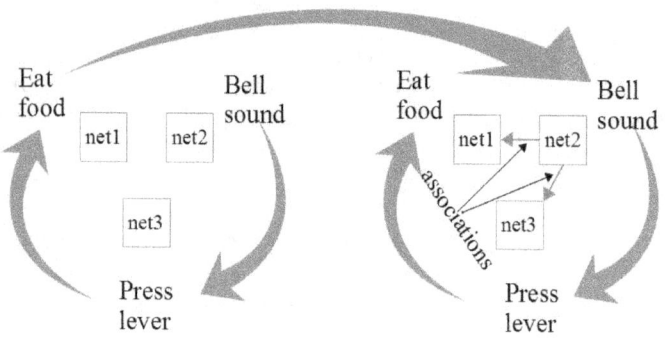

Figure 5.4: Reward based synaptic plasticity example

After some trials, the cat learns that it has to press the lever shortly after the bell sound, to ensure that it would be rewarded. In other words, the cat gradually learns to associate the reward with the bell sound. How does it happen?

The acts of listening to the sound, and the act of pressing the lever, are handled by two separate neural networks in the brain of the cat. To start with, these two networks are unconnected and have no relation to one another. That is why the cat initially keeps pressing the lever even if no sound is heard.

But gradually, a connection builds up between these two networks and that is when the cat automatically performs the act of pressing the lever when it hears the sound. Not only that, the cat also starts salivating on hearing the sound of the bell. That is, it also associates the act of eating with the sound.

What actually happens in the brain is that the reward – food in this case – makes some special neurons to produce some special chemicals that are distributed to various regions in the brain. It is this chemical that induces synaptic connections to be built between two networks that were previously unconnected. How exactly it succeeds in doing that is not well understood.

Both reward and punishment serve to perform similar functions. And we need more research to understand this very commonly observed behavior.

There is yet another way the synapses can get refined in neural networks.

Feedback based synaptic plasticity

When you are learning to play a musical instrument for example, you undergo a series of learning cycles in which you gradually improve your performance till you have mastered the musical instrument. Even here, synaptic plasticity is at work.

For playing a musical instrument, your hand and finger muscles have to operate in a proper coordinated fashion. These muscles are controlled by axons of special neurons – motor neurons – that communicate the signals to these muscles from the brain.

Any ordered sequence of movements of muscles is driven by a collection of neural networks that operate in a sequence in an orderly fashion.

To start with, these networks are 'crude' and will not be in a position to make the proper movement of the fingers. But as you make progress in your learning, these networks keep getting refined so that the movements would be more and more perfect.

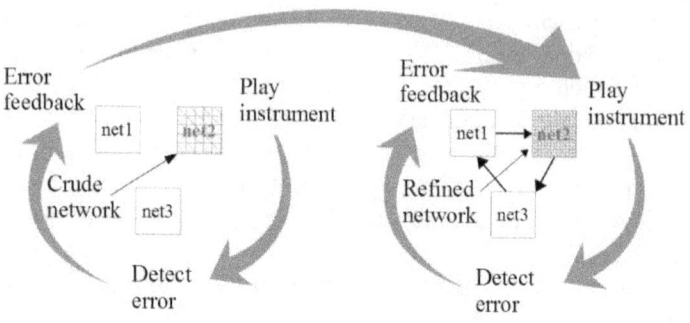

Figure 5.5: Feedback based neural plasticity example

What actually happens is that the 'error feedback' that is given by the sound produced is used to alter the synaptic strengths of these networks so that they are better tuned to do the exact finger movements as needed. This is a trial and error cycle in which the errors are gradually reduced till you become perfect.

Before I move on to the next section, let me briefly explain the analogue of dynamically connected neural networks in the case of a computer.

Dynamically connected networks in a computer

As I said earlier, a computer has several pre-connected networks of transistors each performing a specific function. In a normal computer these networks are fixed and don't change over time. But there are special purpose computers that employ what are called FPGAs (Field Programmable Gate Arrays) to handle special functions that cannot be handled by pre-connected networks.

An FPGA is a pool of gates or blocks of gates that can be dynamically connected or configured as and when the need arises. These interconnections can also be dismantled and reconnected again and again whenever the need changes. That is why they are called 'field programmable'. By connecting these gates, one can implement any function, more efficiently than what can be done by the pre-connected networks.

Many networks are also formed sporadically

There are many networks that keep forming in our brain that may not directly depend on the external inputs. Some of the most interesting cases of sporadic formation of neural networks are the thoughts, imaginations and dreams.

A thought is some sort of 'inner talk'. Imaginations are visualization of scenarios that have no correspondence with external inputs. Dreams are once again visualizations that take place when we are asleep. Added to these there are the not so welcome hallucinations and other mentally created horrors.

None of these have any external input from the external world. Nor do they normally interact with the external world. These are mentally created objects in the form of neural networks. In most cases, these undergo almost similar processing within the brain as if they were generated by external inputs. Each of these may have a different cause.

As of now, we don't have complete understanding of these transient networks that seem to appear from nowhere. Pre stored information in our memories seems to be their source. Most of them appear and disappear without much long term effect.

Some networks may be formed in the process of adaptation

Scientists earlier believed that the pre-connected networks that we inherit at birth remain fixed throughout our lives. But now this opinion seems to be changing. Even the neurons that are part of some pre-connected network —formed as per the genetic blueprint – seem to have the capability to reorganize themselves on rare occasions. This is known as 'neural plasticity'.

Same set of neurons that were earlier performing certain function may join some other network that would be performing altogether different function. Though these are rare occurrences, they do happen and have interesting consequences.

An interesting case of neural plasticity was reported in the case of some people whose limbs had to be amputed for some reason. A person whose arm was amputed previously, started feeling as if his non existing arm – normally called the phantom arm – was touched when actually his face was touched. Similarly someone whose auditory nerves were damaged started hearing a sound when he moved his eyes to some particular position. There were several such cases reported.

What scientists have conjectured, and also confirmed in some cases, is that these cases are the result of neural plasticity. Our brain has a map of our entire body and any touch sensation in a particular part of the body stimulates the neurons in the corresponding part of this map. So the touch is rightly reported. But when an arm is amputed, the neurons in the part of the map that earlier used to respond to touch sensation from the arm are no longer used since they receive no inputs.

What is interesting is that the part of this map corresponding to face lies adjacent to that corresponding to the arm. In rare cases, the unused neurons corresponding to the severed arm join this adjacent area. But this reorganization is not complete at all levels of the brain. So, when the face is touched, these neurons that have remapped to the face area report that the sensation is from the arm – which actually does not exist! The end result is that the touch on the face gets reported as both a touch on the face as well as on the nonexistent arm. Similar thing happens in the other case of the deaf patient hearing a sound.

What interests the scientists more is the fact that our body is capable of remapping even the pre-connected set of neurons – which was earlier assumed to be impossible – to adapt to a changed situation. One interesting consequence of this could be the brain repairing itself when some part of the brain is damaged and neurons from some other part trying to perform the function of the damaged part.

6 A brief overview of the brain anatomy

Describing the brain anatomy in detail may need a complete book. It is also quite nomenclature intensive. In this chapter however, I will only touch upon the essentials that would help us in understanding the later chapters. I will restrict myself to giving a broad view here and take up more anatomical details, as and when needed, later. That will probably offload the reader and help in focusing more on the issues of how, rather than exact location and its nomenclature.

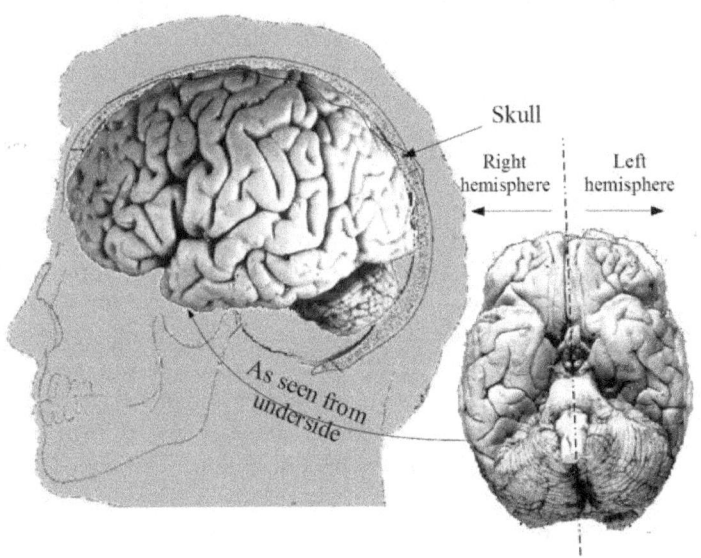

Figure 6.1 Two views of adult human brain

Figure 6.1 shows how an adult human brain looks like. What is shown is the brain of a male person. The brain of a female person is similar. The male brain weighs approximately 1500 grams (around 3 pounds) and that of a female is normally 10% less in weight. It is estimated that an adult brain has something like 10^{12} (1 followed by 12 zeroes!) neurons.

From the underside view of the brain shown in Figure 6.1 you can see two halves of the brain – one on the left and the other in the right. These are called cerebral hemispheres.

Cerebral hemispheres

The brain has two halves – left cerebral hemisphere and right cerebral hemisphere. Normally, the left side of the body is controlled by the right hemisphere and the right side of the body by the left hemisphere.

The outer most 'shell' of these cerebral hemispheres is called cerebral cortex. This is where most of the 'action' takes place. The highly folded surface you see in Figure 6.1 is the cerebral cortex. This is where you find the 'grey matter' and the 'white matter'.

The grey matter are layers of neurons that do most of the computations of the brain and the white matter comprise of bundles of axons that provide connectivity between these neurons. The white matter lies deep inside the cerebral cortex below the layers of neurons.

There are different types of neurons in various layers of the cerebral cortex. These are pre-connected in some way. Some of these implement various pre-defined functions of the brain. Others may act as relay neurons that convey information from one part of the brain to some other part.

A large number of neurons are available as 'spare', that organize themselves as various neural networks during the life time of the person. We will be seeing some of these details in later chapters. Table 6-1 gives some of the numbers related to the cerebral cortex.

Table 6-1 Some cortical numbers

Neuronal density	40000/ mm^3
Synaptic density	8 X 10^8 / mm^3
Synapses per neuron	1000 to 20000
Length of axons	few mm to 1 m
Time duration of spike	~ 1 msec.
Velocity of spike along the axon	~ 120 m/sec

Each hemisphere of the cerebral cortex is divided into four parts called *lobes*. These lobes are frontal lobe, temporal lobe, parietal lobe and occipital lobe. Figure 6.2 shows these lobes.

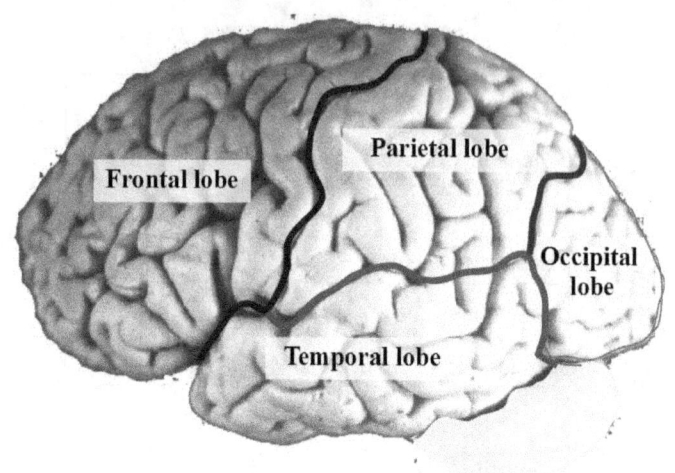

Figure 6.2 Lobes of cerebral cortex

Functional areas of the cerebral cortex

Various regions of the cerebral cortex implement various functionality of the brain.

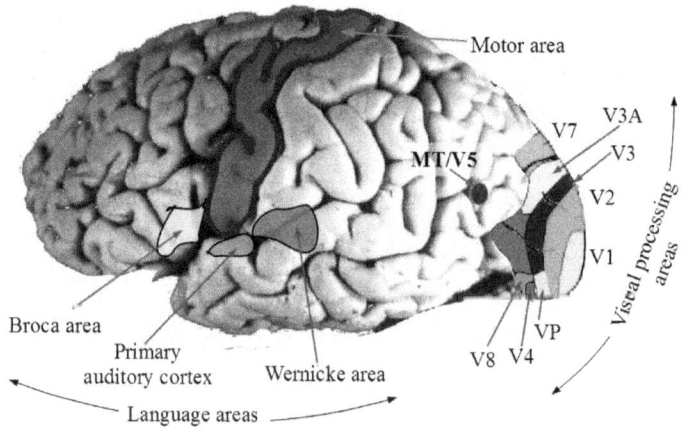

Figure 6.3 Some of the functional areas of cerebral cortex

Figure 6.3 shows some of these regions/areas. We will see more about these areas in later chapters.

The cerebral cortex achieves its functionality in coordination with structures buried deep in the brain. To see these structures we need to take sections of the brain. In the next section we will see such sectional views of the brain.

Brain sectional views

Brain sections are normally depicted as taken along three mutually perpendicular planes. Figure 6.4 shows these three mutually perpendicular planes and the sectional views of the brain along these planes.

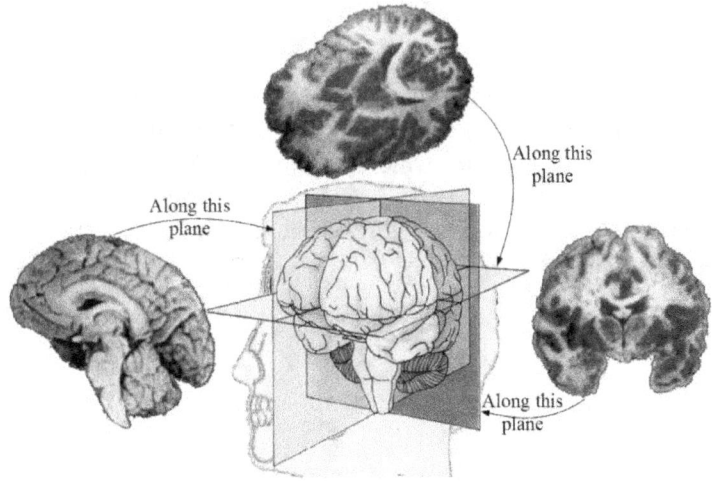

Figure 6.4 Three sectional views of the brain

Let us use one of these sectional views to get a rough idea about some of the structures below the cerebral cortex.

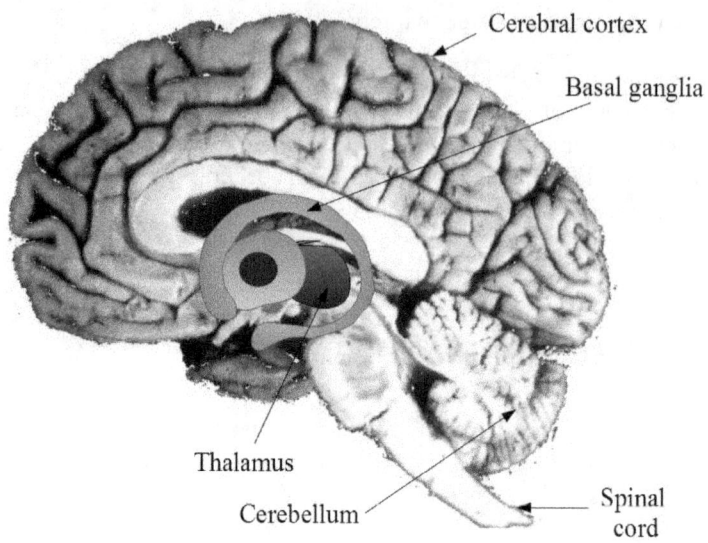

Cerebral cortex

Basal ganglia

Thalamus

Cerebellum

Spinal cord

Figure 6.5 Some important structure inside the brain

Figure 6.5 shows one such sectional view detailing some of the important internal structures. Bear in mind that these are sectional views and the structures which are otherwise three dimensional are shown here as two dimensional shapes. At the moment don't worry about the roles of these structures. I will talk about them later.

7 How does our visual system function?

Most of us are blessed with this wonderful capability of our brain, namely the ability to see things. The sense of vision is of utmost importance to us and we often use it to acquire most of the information from our surroundings. You may be surprised to know that as much as one fourth of our brain is involved in visual processing. That is our main source of information. In the primitive life forms this information is needed either to perceive the external threats or to look for possible sources of food.

In many ways, our visual system is far superior to the most sophisticated computer available today. Naturally, it is also one of the most intensively researched areas when it comes to understanding the functioning of the mind. For several decades scientists have tried to unravel the mystery of various facets of this marvelous functionality. But ironically, even after decades of research, we are still far away from knowing sufficiently about this crucial feat of our mind. We know bits and pieces, some informed guesses, some fantastic theories, and that is about all.

In this chapter, I will discuss some of the interesting things about our visual system, some research findings, and some theories about how it could be working. I definitely don't intend to cover all aspects of the research in this broad area.

Let me start with the point where all the action starts – namely our eyes.

Our eyes are only the windows to our visual system

We see through our eyes. But the eyes are not all. They are just the entry points. In Figure 7.1, I have shown a simple diagram of the eye with its inner details.

When we look at an external object, the light that is reflected from the external object enters our eyes. First this light gets focused into our eyes by the cornea. Cornea does 75% of the focusing. Remaining 25% of the focusing is done by the eye lens that is behind the cornea. This focused light from the external object falls on the retina and creates an image, just like in a camera.

Figure 7.1 Structure of the eye

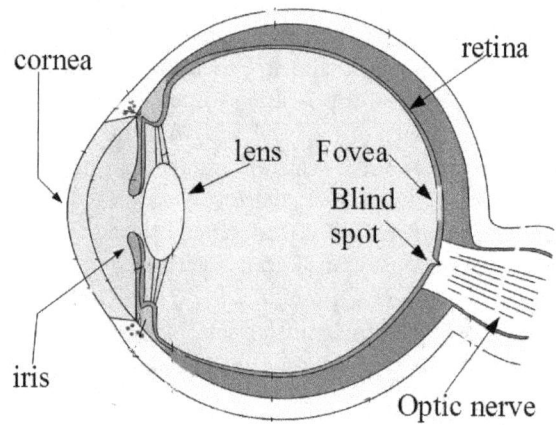

In a camera also we have an aperture, a lens and a film or a photo sensitive material on which the image is captured. The retina is like the film or the photo sensitive material. Exactly like a camera, the image that is captured on the retina is a mirror image. The left portion of the image falls on the right half of the retina and the right portion of the image falls on the left half of the retina.

This retina is actually a massive array of photosensitive neurons - almost 125 millions of them. In the language of digital camera, our eyes are like a digital camera of 125 mega pixels resolution! But unlike the digital camera, this resolution is not uniform. The centre of the retina, i.e. straight opposite the eye lens, has the highest resolution and the resolution gradually decreases when we move away from the centre of the retina.

You probably wonder why this variation? The reason is that you would like to get more details of the part of the image which you are staring at rather than its surroundings. When you stare at an external object, the object's image falls at the centre of the retina and the objects that surround this object fall on either side of the retina. This is also the reason why your vision blurs on either side of your gaze, where as straight ahead you get a clear picture.

How is the image captured?

The retina is a three layered structure as shown in Figure 7.2. The top layer (layer 1) has what are known as ganglion cells (a kind of neurons) that collect information from the second layer of neurons, which in turn collect the signals from the bottom most layer.

The light that is focused on the retina passes through these layers and finally reaches the bottom most layer that has photosensitive neurons called rods and cones.

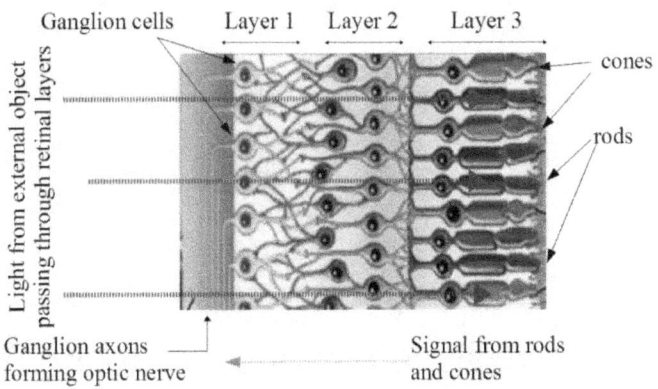

Figure 7.2 Cross section of retina

These special neurons convert the light energy into electrical signals that they pass backwards to the top layer through the intermediate layer.

The rods are sensitive to dim light and don't differentiate between colors. On the other hand, the cones are sensitive to bright light, both monochrome as well as colored. There are three types of cones, each sensitive to a range of light frequencies. As you know, the color of light depends on its frequency. So, these three types of cones convey three different ranges of colors and effectively convey all the varieties of colors that we are capable of seeing.

Interestingly, even our computers use three colors – Red, Green and Blue (RGB) – to convey all the colors that we see on the computer screens. Various combinations of these three colors in different proportions convey different colors.

The passing of signals from these rods and cones to the neurons in the next layer is not uniform. At the centre of the retina, each rod and cone sends signals to the next layer, whereas as we move away from the centre, the information is collected from multiple rods and cones. Effectively, the centre of the retina collects information with high resolution and this resolution decreases as we move on either side.

Finally, the captured image on the retina is conveyed to rest of the brain through what is called the optic nerve. Actually, the optic nerve is not a single nerve but a bundle of millions of axons coming out of the ganglion neurons in the top layer of the retina. The point where the optic nerve gets connected to the retina is devoid of neurons and hence is insensitive to light. This is what is called 'blind spot' where no image is captured.

Some preprocessing takes place before the image leaves the retina through the optic nerve. But I will skip those details here and go ahead for more interesting things.

Actual processing takes place in the visual cortex

Eyes are just input devices like the I/O devices of our computer. They do some processing but pass on most of the information to the brain for further processing. The place in the brain where most of the action takes place is called the visual cortex, a region of cerebral cortex. Before the image reaches the visual cortex, it passes through some brain areas as shown in Figure 7.3.

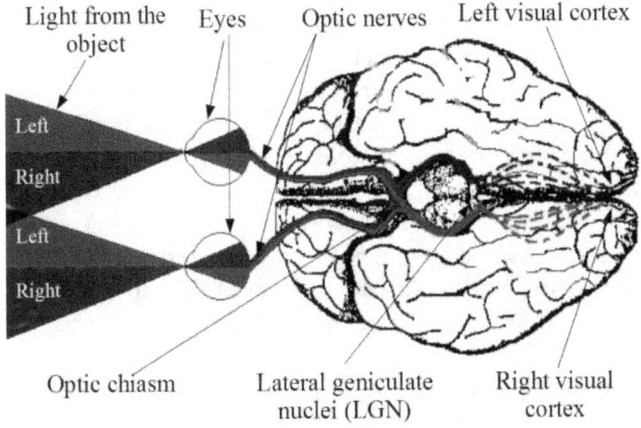

Figure 7.3 Transmission of captured image to the visual cortex (underside view)

As I said earlier, the external object forms a mirror image on the retina. That means, the light from the left side of the object falls on the right side of the retina and vice versa. This happens in both the eyes. This is what I have shown in Figure 7.3 by using two colors and marking them as 'left' and 'right'.

Two sides of the image from each eye are conveyed to the brain through the optic nerve. At a point known as 'optic chiasm' these nerves cross each other and all the axons corresponding to one side from each eye are grouped together. Further down, the axons corresponding to the left sides of both the eyes are connected to right lateral geniculate nucleus (right LGN) and those from the right sides are connected to the left lateral geniculate nucleus (left LGN).

The image from each of the geniculate nuclei is further conveyed to the area V1 of the visual cortex (shown later in Figure 7.4) through appropriate connections between the neurons in the intermediate stages. The left LGN conveys the information to the left visual cortex and the right LGN conveys the information to the right visual cortex. These connections are such that 'spacial order' between the image regions from each eye is maintained. That means regions of the retina map on to exactly corresponding regions of the visual cortex.

"Where" and "What" of visual processing

As I said earlier, as much as one fourth of our brain is involved in visual processing. What exactly our brain does by processing the inputs form our eyes? The fundamental question is - why do we see? We tend to think that the purpose of our vision is to acquire information about the world around us. But what use is this information?

There are mainly two purposes. Firstly, we want to see so that we can take appropriate physical actions depending on what we see. This is what the scientists term as "vision for action". The other main purpose is to gather information about objects so that this information can later be used for mental planning – i.e. "vision for perception".

These two types of visual activities involve distinct processing. The first one namely "vision for action" is more concerned with precise location of the object, its exact shape, dimensions, the way it is oriented, and its movements if any. In other words, it is more about "where" aspect of the object that is being seen.

The second one namely "vision for perception" is more interested in acquiring general information about the objects with the primary aim of distinguishing it or matching it with objects previously seen. The location of the object, its orientation, movement, and size are not much of importance in this case.

These two aspects of vision are generally termed as "where" and "what" of vision. Now the important question is how are these two aspects of vision handled by the visual cortex? Is there a single region where both these are handled, or are there more than one region?

The "two steams" hypothesis

During the 1980s scientists had identified that there are two distinct streams in the cortex of macaque monkeys that processed visual inputs. Both these streams originated in the primary visual cortex. One of them called the "ventral stream" spanned various regions starting from primary visual cortex to the inferior temporal cortex (IT cortex) and the other one called the "dorsal stream" spanned from the primary visual cortex to the posterior parietal cortex. These two streams seem to process different aspects of the visual inputs. But what was not clear was whether similar streams existed in human brains as well.

Ten years later, two scientists namely Goodale and Milner studied two patients who had their visual cortex damaged for some reason. One of them, referred to as R.V., had lesions in the regions spanning primary visual cortex to the inferior parietal lobe and the other one, referred to as D.F., had damage in the regions corresponding to the ventral stream.

R.V. could identify the objects shown to her but could not make accurate hand and finger movements to hold irregularly shaped objects. The problem was not in her hand or finger movements but with the inability to make judgments about the movement based on the visual information about the objects. R.V. could however, hold the objects once the objects were touched and felt.

On the other hand, D.F. had no difficulty in accurately holding the irregularly shaped objects purely based on visual clues, but failed to differentiate between different objects. In other words, D.F. had problem identifying the objects.

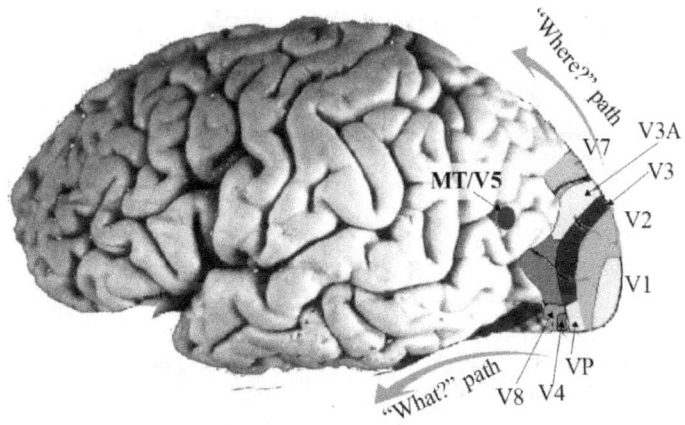

Figure 7.4 Visual processing regions of the visual cortex (side view)

These observations and the previous work on macaque monkeys prompted Goodale and Milner to come up with the hypothesis that there exist two distinct pathways in the human brain that processed object identification – "What aspect", and the visually guided action planning – "Where aspect" of the objects seen.

These two pathways are often termed as the "ventral stream" or the "What path" and the "dorsal stream" or the "Where path" of visual processing and these are as shown in Figure 7.4.

Both these paths take inputs from primary visual cortex. Each of the regions on the path is denoted by the letter 'V' suffixed by a number. Some of these areas are shown in Figure 7.4 as V1, V2 and so on. V1 is the region where the image processing starts. This is where the signals from the lateral geniculate nucleus land before they get processed further.

Though we have broad idea of the kind of processing that takes place in each of these areas, we are yet to know exact details of how those processing are done. There are several theories proposed by various groups of scientists and some of these theories are validated (to some extent) using computer simulations. In the next section, I will give the underlying ideas behind one such theory about object identification.

How do we identify objects?

In Chapter 4 we saw some simple neural networks that can recognize simple patterns. But recognizing real life objects is far more difficult than that. Several things can make this recognition a highly complex process.

When you look at a face for example, if it is a known face we generally identify it even if the face is turned in different directions, irrespective of how the face is illuminated, independent of the distance (to some extent) between that face and us, independent of the facial expressions and so on. A simple neural network that is setup to recognize a face under ideal conditions cannot take into account all these variations that may mislead it. Added to that, there is the problem of clutter – the objects around the face - that may make the face less noticeable.

So, object recognition is not as simple as what we tend to think. Before a neural network can recognize an object, the object needs to be brought into some 'standard' form that is independent of all the variations I listed above. The neural network can then handle minor variations and do the recognition job once such invariance to transformations is achieved.

Let me take a simpler example. Consider various numbers on a panel as shown on the left side of Figure 7.5. Some of the numbers are turned in various directions. Also, the sizes of the numbers are not the same. To make the matter worse, these numbers are scattered all over the panel.

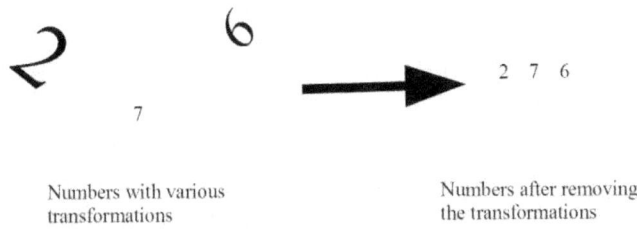

Numbers with various
transformations

Numbers after removing
the transformations

Figure 7.5 Recognizing transformed objects

This probably reminds you the 'word challenge' often used by various internet sites to confirm that you are indeed some human being and not some program that is trying to access the site. The idea behind such word challenges is that an automated program cannot recognize the letters in the word that are transformed in all possible ways. But we – human beings – can still recognize the letters ignoring all variations.

How does our mind achieve this feat? This apparently simple capability of our mind is yet to be understood completely by the scientists. One theory is that our brain 'undoes' various transformations in a step by step fashion before doing the recognition. It is as if the numbers on the left side of Figure 7.5 are translated to the numbers shown on the right side. Note that the numbers shown on the right are size invariant, rotation invariant and also position invariant.

Though our brain does not really perform such a translation, the processing is such that it effectively results in a view of the objects that are free of all transformations that make the recognition difficult. The neural networks that are setup to recognize the objects can then easily do their job without getting distracted by the transformations.

How does the visual cortex achieve this?

As I said earlier, visual cortex is the region of the brain in which visual processing is performed. The actual object recognition takes place in the inferior temporal cortex (IT cortex) that is left end of the "What" path as shown in the Figure 7.4. Before the object can be recognized, the brain has to 'undo' all the transformations that the objects have undergone. Scientists theorize that the regions V1, V2 and V4 of the visual cortex do this job.

Object recognition process has two mutually conflicting requirements to meet.

1. It has to differentiate fine differences between different objects: 'selectivity', and

2. ignore minor variations in a given object: 'invariance'.

These requirements are met by a hierarchy of neural networks that alternately try to satisfy both these requirement at each stage. These neural networks are supposed to be present in regions V1 to V4.

At the bottom of the hierarchy, the networks handle small regions of the captured image and as we go higher in the hierarchy, the outputs of the lower level get combined to cover larger and larger areas of the captured image.

The processing starts with simple networks that identify tiny fragments of edges in the images. These networks are setup in such a way that they recognize an edge by ignoring minor tilts in the edge. The next level networks combine the outputs of these lower level networks so that larger sized edges which are also tolerant of minor rotations are recognized. At further higher level, the networks achieve immunity to other transformations such as illumination, magnification and so on. Whole lot of previously acquired information and clues about the objects is used in doing these transformations.

At the lowest level, the neural networks are setup to recognize simple edges, an act that is almost independent of the actual object types. But as we move higher in the hierarchy, the networks are setup based on prior exposure to edges of various objects and they capture the typical properties of the objects often encountered. There is also a learning that goes on to alter the networks to account for the new transformations encountered in the process of recognition.

Finally, when the signals reach the IT cortex, we have the images that are free of transformations and are ready to be recognized. This is roughly how the scientists theorize the working of the visual cortex as far as the object recognition is concerned.

The role of attention in object recognition

In real life, we normally pay attention to what we see and our attention can alter the process of recognition. We may focus our attention on a particular region of the captured image, observe it closely, and so on. The attention also plays a crucial role when we want to look for a specific object instead of just identify the objects in front of us.

Mere object recognition process moves from V1 to all the way up to IT cortex. Whereas looking for a specific object is an activity that is driven from the top and it influences the recognition process down the line.

The role of attention adds further complexity to the act of object recognition. Various scientists have proposed theories about how attention works in coordination with the recognition process. I will not go into those details here. It suffices to say that object recognition is not as simple as we tend to think and is yet to be fully understood.

I will skip the processing that takes place on the other path namely 'the where path' for brevity.

8 How do we remember things?

Just imagine how we would have been if we did not have the capability to remember things!. All of us have experienced the confusion caused by temporary forgetfulness, more so as we age. Living without being able to remember is almost impossible!

Most of us are familiar with computer memories, but have you ever wondered how we remember things? I did discuss very briefly in Chapter 4 the basic mechanisms that may underlie memory in our brains. In this chapter, I will elaborate a bit more and discuss some of the interesting aspects of memory.

Quest for understanding memory

Way back in 1950s scientists debated on whether the brain as a whole worked on various aspects of the mind or different specialized regions of the brain worked on different aspects. As far as the storage of memory is concerned, it was not clear whether it is done in a specific part of the brain or the brain as a whole contributes to memory.

At the same time some peculiar cases of patients suffering from amnesia came to light. What was common in all these patients was that some specific parts of their brain were earlier removed for medical reasons. The most often quoted case was that of one Mr. H.M.

H.M. and his strange memory problem

H.M. had his medial temporal lobe removed as a remedy for the epileptic seizures he used to suffer. As a result of the surgery, he was freed of his seizures but he seemed to have severe problems with remembering things. But interestingly, his other intellectual abilities did not seem to get affected. In fact, he scored higher on IQ tests, after surgery.

H.M. could remember ongoing things as long as he focused his attention on them. But he forgot them as soon as his attention was diverted. For example, H.M. could remember a given 3 digit number for as long as 15 minutes if he focused his attention on the number by playing with the digits. But as soon as his attention was diverted, he totally forgot the number.

H.M. had other memory related problems. Even though he could clearly remember his childhood experiences, he had serious problem remembering day today events. He could not even identify the people whom he routinely met.

Though H.M. could remember events that happened several years before the surgery, events that happened a few years or months before the surgery were forgotten.

If H.M. was shown some object and the same object was shown once again after a short delay, H.M. was unable to say whether he had ever seen that object. But if this delay is reduced to almost zero, he could recollect having seen the object. That means, whatever he newly remembered seemed to vanish after a short delay.

Scientists performed several tests on H.M. In one such test, H.M. was shown pictures of objects with some parts removed. H.M. was asked to identify the objects. Initially, with most parts removed, H.M., like any other normal person, could not identify the object. But as more and more deleted parts were added back, H.M. could identify the object. When this experiment was repeated with the same set of objects previously shown, H.M. performed better even though he did not remember going through the experiment before.

When the experiment was repeated with the same set of objects even after one hour, H.M. could perform surprisingly better than before. That means he could take advantage of earlier exposures to the objects. But what is interesting is that H.M. could not consciously recollect that he had ever seen those objects! For him, it was his first exposure to the object, as if. But his brain somehow seemed to have learnt from the previous exposure to the object.

In yet another test, H.M. was trained in some picture drawing task. The task was to draw a line between two concentric stars as shown in Figure 8.1. It is an easy task. But the difficulty comes when the line has to be drawn not by directly looking at the picture but while looking at the image of the picture reflected in a mirror kept in front of the picture. Even normal people need several rounds of training to perform this task since the mirror image always confuses the hand movements.

Figure 8.1 Star drawing task

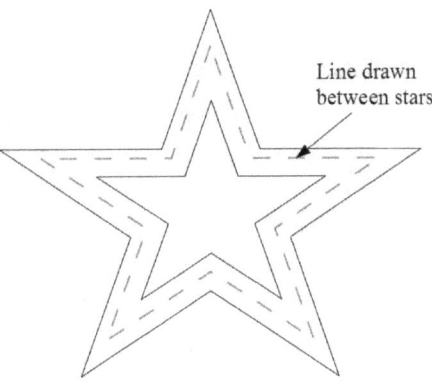

Line drawn between stars

But surprisingly H.M. could learn this task, like any other normal person, He could, after some training, draw the line between the stars without much difficulty. But he did not remember that he was ever trained in this task. He had acquired a new skill but he forgot how he acquired it! He knew how to do the task but did not know that he knew it!

What do all these observations point to?

There are not one but many types of memories

The experiments that were performed on H.M. and consequent observations seemed to hint that there is more than one type of memory in our mind. The following observations lead to this conclusion.

1. Let us start with the observation that H.M. could remember things as long as his attention remained focused on the ob-

ject. He forgot the object as soon as his attention was diverted to something else. This means that there is some form of memory that remains active as long as it is continuously accessed and seems to get erased or replaced by another object to which the attention is diverted.

2. H.M. could recollect the events that were stored in the memory several years ago, even when these events were not continuously accessed. That means that this memory has a long term existence and does not easily fade away.

3. At the same time, there were other events that were stored in his memory months or a few years before his surgery, which were completely unavailable after the surgery. What it could mean is that these events were stored in the parts of his brain that were removed during surgery.

4. Assuming that these kinds of events were similar in nature to those others which were stored several years ago, but were still available, it is possible that memory contents get transferred from one location of the brain to another over a period of time.

Let us next come to H.M.'s ability to learn new motor skills such as drawing a line between two concentric stars while looking at the mirror image. H.M. like normal people could learn the new skill after some training. He could perform the task, but could not remember the event that he had learnt that skill. What does that mean?

1. It means that the memory of operations to be performed while doing some manual task is stored in some region of the brain which is different from the region which was surgically removed.

2. This memory could be used for performing the task, but cannot be recalled in the normal way other events can be recalled. In other words, this memory is not explicitly available for access. This memory is not about any event but about the step by step procedure of drawing the line.

3. The fact that H.M. has learnt a new skill but does not remember having learnt it, means that the memory of having learnt something – an event - is stored in a different part of the brain which happens to be the part that was surgically removed.

H.M.'s ability to recognize the objects whose parts were removed and then added one by one indicates that H.M.'s brain could remember previous exposures to the partial object even though H.M. was not aware of this memory. It is as if the previous exposures to the object somehow 'primed' his memory so that that information could be used to recognize the object faster than before. And this priming must be taking place in some part of the brain which was not surgically removed.

All these observations lead to the conclusion that there are different types of memories. The differences in the memory could be based on

1. Life time of the memory
2. Use of memory
3. Part of the brain in which it is stored

Accordingly, we have

1. Short term memories, medium term memories, long term memories - based on the life time of memory.
2. Explicitly accessible memories about events and facts (also called declarative memory), implicitly accessible memory of performing some task (also called procedural memory), implicitly used memory to store previously gathered partial information (called priming) – based on usage of memory.
3. Memories that are stored in different regions of the brain – based on where the memory is stored.

Further investigation led the scientists to classify the memories as shown in Figure 8.2.

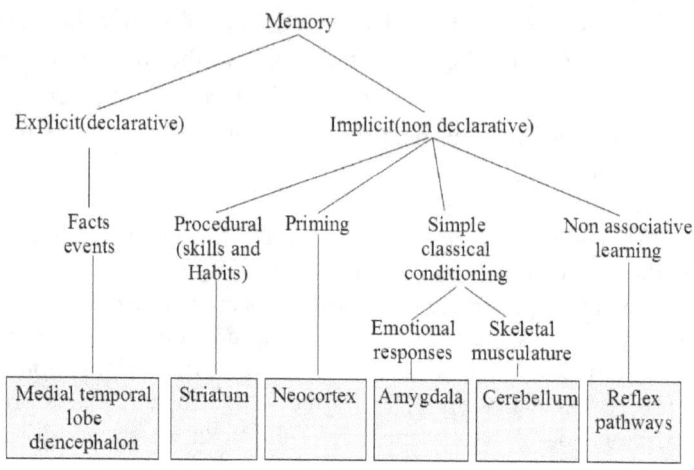

Figure 8.2 Different types of memories and their location

If you are familiar with computer memory system, you probably identify conceptual similarities between the memory system in our brains and those in a computer.

Memory systems in a computer (you can skip this if you choose to)

Though the physical implementation of a computer memory and the memory in our brains differ, conceptually they have several similarities. A closer look at the working of a computer memory may give some additional insights into the memory systems in our brain.

Figure 8.3 shows physical organization of computer memory.

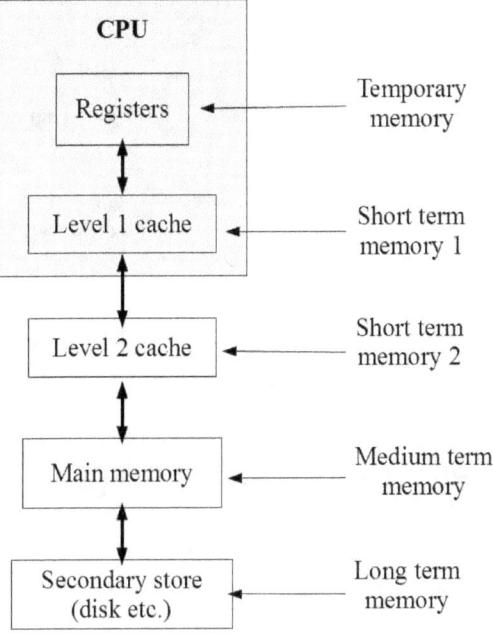

Figure 8.3 Computer memory system (physical)

Looked at from the point of view of usage, computer memory can be seen as shown in Figure 8.4.

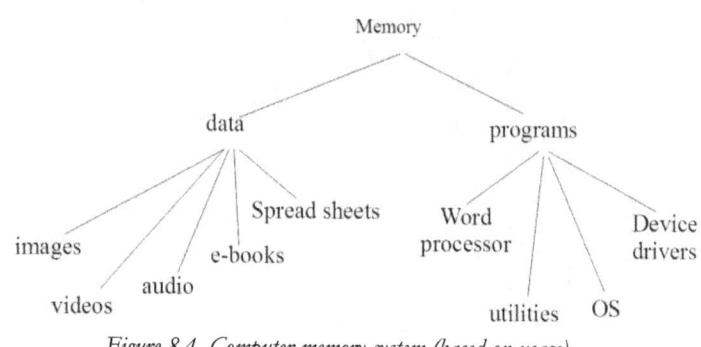

Figure 8.4 Computer memory system (based on usage)

Memories are formed in stages

For more than one reason, our lasting memories are not formed instantaneously but in stages and this process may span several years.

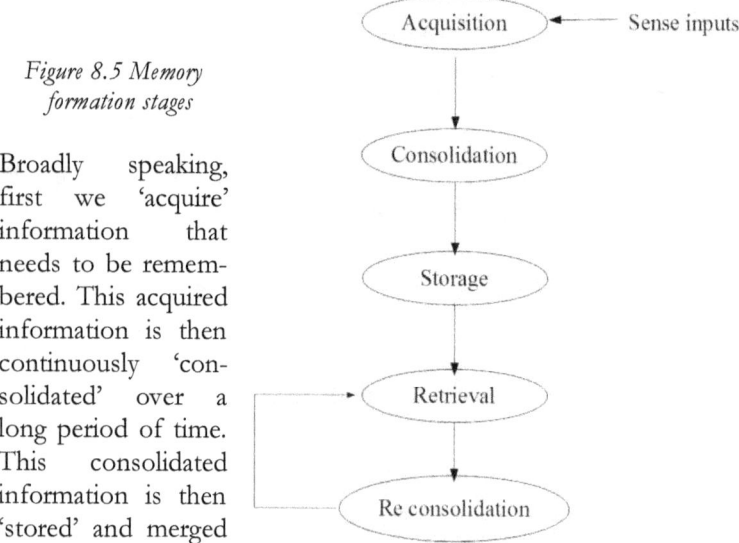

Figure 8.5 Memory formation stages

Broadly speaking, first we 'acquire' information that needs to be remembered. This acquired information is then continuously 'consolidated' over a long period of time. This consolidated information is then 'stored' and merged with other previously stored information in the brain. This stored information is subsequently 'retrieved' as and when needed. In the process of retrieval these stored information may undergo changes or give rise to newer information in a process called 'reconsolidation'. Let us briefly see each of these stages.

104

Stage 1: Memory acquisition

The information that is acquired and later stored in memory normally comes from sense inputs. This acquisition may take place in different parts of the brain. This acquired information would be in terms of a cluster of neurons – generally called 'neural cliques' - that continuously fire in response to the external inputs. The rate of firing of these neurons depends on variety of things. Emotionally charged events such as a threat perception are known to produce a highly active cluster of neurons, each of which fire at a very rapid rate.

The firing also gets boosted when continuous attention is paid to the event that caused the formation of these neural clusters. The formation of these clusters is very quick and happens in real-time. But left to itself, the activity of the neurons in such an active neural cluster would gradually die down, making the acquired information to be lost.

But in normal cases this does not happen. The memory is retained over prolonged period even in the absence of external inputs and attention, due to the process of consolidation.

Stage 2: Memory consolidation

There is always some 'default' interconnection between the neurons in the neural clusters that hold the acquired information. But these connections and their synaptic strengths are general and not specific to the particular information that is acquired. These strengths need to be varied to form a network that is specific to the acquired information that needs to be remembered. Or in other words, the information needs to be 'encoded' within the neural network as a structural property. This is what happens in the consolidation stage. This process of consolidation may go on for months or even years before the memory is finally stored as long term memory for later use.

There are other things that happen during consolidation of memory. The acquired information is 'encoded' in such a manner that only essential things are retained. Also, there is also an attempt to abstract out things based on generality between other such events. This capability to abstract out information is what gives us the ability to store enormous amounts of information in our mind. The process of abstraction moves the acquired information from a set of specific events to a set of general events and inferences based on those events.

One of the important structures in the medial temporal lobe, namely the hippocampus, plays a crucial role in this memory consolidation. If you recall H.M.'s case, this consolidation was not happening in his brain since his medial temporal lobe was surgically removed. The sudden absence of hippocampus prevented previously acquired information from consolidating further and hence that information was lost. As a result, not only he forgot things once his attention was diverted from the information that was acquired, but also all that information that was in the process of consolidation for several months before the surgery.

Stage 3: Memory storage

After sufficiently being consolidated, the information is finally transferred to other permanent areas in the cortex. While doing so, the newly acquired and consolidated information is 'linked' to other information that are previously stored. This forms the long term memory that may potentially be retained forever. Since this region where the memory is stored finally, was intact in H.M., he could remember the events that happened several years before the surgery.

This stored information may be retrieved as and when needed.

Stage 4: Memory retrieval and re-consolidation

Memories are retrieved either directly or indirectly when associated memories are retrieved. Some scientists are of the opinion that retrieved memories are in the same unstable state as newly acquired memories and they need to be re-consolidated. What could also be possible is that new memories get formed as a result of the retrieved information. And these newly formed memories need to be consolidated. Alternatively, when memories are retrieved, the brain may further filter out information that may not be useful over a long term or encode the information further to abstract out the details.

If you compare the formation of memories in the brain with that in a computer, you can see several conceptual similarities.

Formation of memories in a computer (you can skip this)

Here I am using the word 'memory' to refer to the information stored and not the physical device in which it is stored.

Refer to Figure 8.3 where I have outlined the physical memory organization in a computer. The memory starts getting formed in the registers. A register may 'acquire' information either from an I/O port (similar to sense inputs in the brain), or from previously 'stored' memory, or information that is formed as a result of some operation.

For example, when you add A to B to get the result C, A and B are temporarily held in two registers. These are added and the result of addition is moved to another register. The storage of this information in these registers is temporary. As long as A, B and C are being used; they may remain in the registers. When they are no longer used, either they are simply replaced by some other information or are just discarded. This is conceptually similar to attention being needed to retain newly acquired information.

If the newly computed result is useful later, it is moved to next stage of memory namely the level 1 cache. This result remains in level 1 cache as long as it is needed or when the location it occupies in the level 1 cache needs to be overwritten. The information that is needed for a longer term would then move to level 2 cache. The process continues and the information, if useful, moves to main memory and finally to disk. Once it reaches the disk it becomes almost permanent.

A couple of things need to be noted. The memories at a higher level are faster than those in the lower level, but are also limited in capacity. The life time of the information stored in them is also less compared to that of the information stored at lower levels of memory.

Further, as information moves from higher stage to lower stage, many of the temporarily useful information is discarded retaining only those that have a long term value. Structurally too, the information becomes more and more abstract as it moves to lower levels of memory. At the register level, they may be just some numbers, whereas when they reach the disk, they may represent information stored in some spread sheet or some relational database, for example. Long term storage also 'associates' the newly stored information with that which is previously stored.

When it comes to retrieval of stored information, the retrieved information moves up the hierarchy and may appear like newly acquired information. But at least in the computer, retrieval does not change the stored state of the information. What changes is the newly formed information which is formed using the retrieved information. The operations performed on the retrieved information may indirectly change the previously stored information more as a result of deletion of the previously stored information and replacing it with newly formed information.

In a computer, the memory formation is purely an electronic or electromagnetic phenomenon. But how does the memory work in our brains?

As I discussed in Chapter 5 and later in Chapter 6, the neurons in our brain are pre-connected at the initial developmental stage. Some of these are pre-connected to perform different specialized functions. Others are pre-connected in possibly random fashion. Now the intriguing question is how do these randomly connected neurons store memory?

At least in lower level animals, scientists found that these interconnections are almost the same irrespective of learning undergone by the animal. That being the case, how is information stored in these pre-connected networks? What in these networks changes as the animal learns or remembers new things?

Synaptic plasticity seems to be the under-lying mechanism

In Chapter 4, we have seen that the functionality of a neural network depends not only on the interconnections between the neurons in the network but most importantly on the relative strengths of these connections – or in other words the synaptic strengths.

Now it may look obvious to us that the memory is also stored by suitably changing the synaptic strengths in some pre-connected neural networks representing the memory. But it took several decades for the scientists to arrive at that conclusion.

Way back in 1970s, Eric Kandel and his co-scientists were trying to understand how memory is formed in our brain. Since understanding the functioning of a brain that contained trillions of neurons connected in a complex fashion was formidable, they were looking for simpler alternatives. They felt that if they could study the basic mechanisms in simpler animals with fewer neurons, they may be in a position to extrapolate the findings to the working of the human brain.

They chose giant marine snails for this purpose. The advantage of this choice was that the snail had very few neurons – of the order of thousands (around 20000) – and most neural circuits had few hundred neurons. The sizes of some of these neurons were so large (almost 1 mm.) that they could be seen by naked eye. They had distinct pigmentation making them easily identifiable. These neurons were large enough to dissect, to view the internal changes and also to inject various chemicals to study their effects.

These scientists performed several experiments to study how some reflex actions – withdrawal of the gill upon stimulation of the siphon - are learnt and remembered in these neural networks. Their observations were quite interesting.

They found that even though the interconnections between the neurons did not change, the learnt information – memory – was stored by altering the relative strengths of the interconnections – synaptic strengths. This synaptic strength could either increase or decrease depending on what is learnt. Further, these altered strengths persisted over long periods of time. The duration of this persistence depended on the nature of learning.

This variation of the synaptic strength is called synaptic plasticity. This synaptic plasticity is what Donald Hebb speculated way back in 1949 (I discussed this in Chapter 5). There are several mechanisms that alter these synaptic strengths. Each mechanism comes to play at certain stage of memory formation.

In the early stages, there is a temporary change in the synaptic strength based on the co-activity of two interconnected neurons. This change lasts only for a short time. Whenever two interconnected neurons fire together, there are some chemical messages that get transmitted from the post-synaptic neuron back to the synapse that is connected to its dendrite. Even though the synaptic contact may not be strong enough to excite the post-synaptic neuron on its own at that time, the very fact that the pre-synaptic and post-synaptic neurons have fired together results in temporary changes in the synapse so that its strength temporarily increases. But this increase in synaptic strength – though quick - does not last long.

Longer lasting synaptic strength changes require production of some special proteins which takes some time. Simultaneously some genes also get activated and over a period of time, not only the strengths of the synapses increase, but also new synaptic connections between the pre and post-synaptic neurons get formed. This makes the memory long lasting.

Why is memory formed in stages?

You probably wonder why the memory is formed in stages and not instantaneously. The stage wise formation of the memory is due to mainly two reasons. Firstly, the chemical changes needed, the production of proteins, and the activation of genes take varying amounts of time. The initially listed processes taking lesser time as compared to those listed later.

Secondly, this staggered consolidation process gives ample time for the brain to weed out unnecessary information and retain only the essential information in a compact and abstract form. If you go back and compare with the memory formation in a computer, you probably would see lot of parallels.

9 Our ability to understand language

Probably one of the things that set us apart from the rest of the beings is our ability to communicate through a well developed language. It is not that other beings don't communicate. They do, in their own way. But their vocabulary is not as intricate as ours. Birds for example, can make elaborate sounds to communicate with each other. Our own pets such as dogs, though unable to communicate much verbally, do understand most of what we tell them. But human abilities, both in terms of speech and understanding of the language, excel rest of the animal world. And that is exactly what makes it difficult for us to use animal models in our attempts to understand our language processing abilities.

What is a language?

In general, language is a means by which we communicate our thoughts to another person. Often it is a transformation of our thoughts into a series of sounds. This series of sounds gets converted back into thoughts at the listener end. It could also be transformation of thoughts into a sequence of written words, as for example, this book you are reading right now. I have translated my thoughts into a sequence of words which you read and translate back into thoughts once again.

In the former case, we communicate through the sense of hearing, and in the latter we use our visual sense. In the extreme case we could also communicate our thoughts through bodily gestures, as in the case of sign language used by people who cannot speak/hear. In all these cases there is an underlying language. The exact mode of expression may be different.

Consequently, communication through language involves a motor output – speech, writing, making gestures and so on; a sense input – sounds, words read, gestures shown, and so on; in addition to the intervening processing which is purely a mental activity.

In this chapter, I will restrict myself to this mental activity which happens to be a part of understanding or producing speech. In particular, I will talk mostly about understanding part of the language, though the other part is equally interesting.

This mental activity of language processing starts once our input system – hearing, vision – captures the communicated message.

What happens to the information communicated? How does our mind understand what the other person is trying to communicate? Remember that this communication is far from perfect. The thoughts of the speaker are rarely communicated in the entirety to the listener. The problem could be the poor communication skills of the speaker or poor comprehending capability of the listener. That apart, how does this processing take place?

What is involved in processing language?

If we take spoken speech as the means through which the ideas are conveyed, the speech is a continuous stream of sounds with or without intervening pauses. If you do not understand Chinese language for example, a Chinese speaker may sound like making some meaningless sequence of sounds with no structure. To understand speech, it needs to be processed at various levels.

At the lowest level, a spoken speech has words that are uttered in a specific sequence. These words could be nouns, verbs, conjuncts and so on. So the first step is to separate this stream of sounds into words. For example, a stream such as 'hewenttoschool' may not make much sense unless we divide this stream into 'he went to school'. In the spoken speech we do it by recognizing the pauses – if there are any – or the change of tone. In written stream we use white spaces and punctuations to do the same job.

Sometimes, there could be more than one way of splitting a given stream into words. For example, the stream 'stuffheknows', when uttered, could either mean 'stuff he knows' or 'stuffy nose'. Depending on how the words are split, the meanings can be different.

Once we separate the words, we need to 'categorize' them as nouns, verbs etc. This phase of language processing that involves splitting into words and categorizing these words is called 'lexical analysis '.

Every language has a specific allowed way of organizing the words to convey meaning. We call this as grammar of that language. Only certain arrangement of words is valid. Others are not allowed. This step of checking whether the given stream of words conforms to grammatical rules is called 'syntactic analysis '.

Not all grammatically correct sentences are meaningful. For example, the sentence "He ate to school" is meaningless even though it is grammatically correct. To be meaningful, the sentence has to convey semantically correct information. Checking whether a given sentence conveys valid meaning is called 'semantic analysis '.

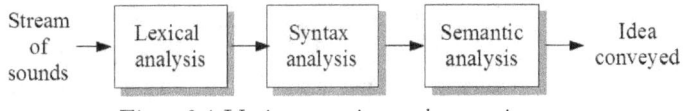

Figure 9.1 Various steps in speech processing

Each of the steps listed above are complex in themselves. To add to the complexity, several nuances in our spoken communication can make the task even more difficult.

Top down or bottom up?

It is not always case that we start with sounds, split them into words and build a grammatically correct and meaningful sequence of words before we understand what is communicated – an approach often referred to as bottom up approach.

On several occasions we do guess as to what is conveyed and use that guess to guide the lexical analysis as well as the syntax and semantic analysis. For example, in a sentence like "Light that candle", you may have to wait till you hear the end of the sentence to decide whether the word 'light' is a noun or a verb. Similarly, whether the word 'that' refers to 'light' or 'candle' will be known only after you hear the complete sentence. This is generally referred to as top down approach.

In general, speech comprehension involves both top down as well as bottom up approaches.

Nested constructs, implied meanings and context sensitivity can make things complex

Sentences can have complex constructs involving arbitrary nesting of phrases and qualifiers. For example, we can construct a sentence such as 'He ate the pie that was made by the old lady who lives in the house behind the bridge'. This sentence has more than one noun and verb. Actually, in this case there are more than one grammatically correct sentences/phrases embedded in a single sentence. This embedding can be arbitrarily long and nested in a complex fashion, making the meaning evident only when one reaches the end of the sentence.

Understanding the speech has added problems in the context of similes, metaphors and other implied meanings. In general, the meaning of a sentence may depend on the context in which it is uttered, the body language of the speaker, our impression about the intention of the speaker and so on.

So, speech is not just a sequence of words. It is much more than that. What is conveyed depends on whole lot of things that may not be evident from the words.

It may be illuminating to know how computers understand language.

How does a computer understand language?
(You may skip this if you choose to)

The language I am talking about here is the programming language that is used to give instructions to the computer.

Computers process language using a program called compiler. A complier translates a sequence of instructions written in a 'high level' language to a 'low level' machine code that can be understood by the computer. The high level description is like the spoken sentences and the machine code is like the thoughts that are the meaning of high level descriptions.

Computer programs are normally written in languages called context free languages. These languages are high level in the sense that the descriptions in these languages can be understood by human beings. These descriptions have to be translated into computer understandable 'code'. This is done by various stages of a compiler as shown in Figure 9.2.

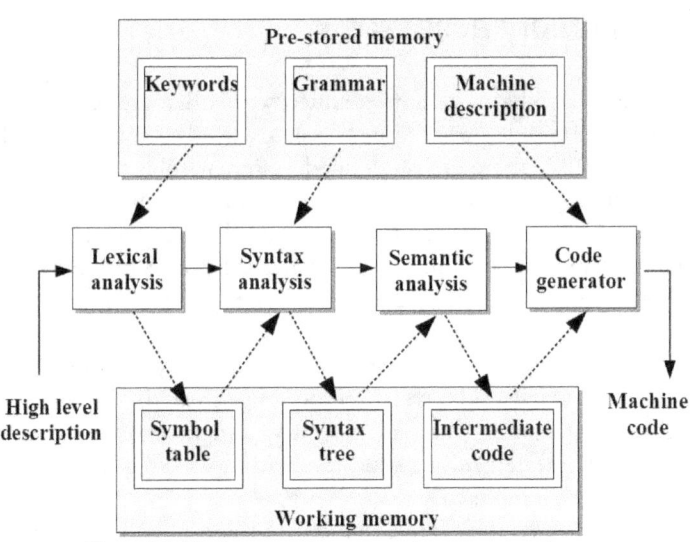

Figure 9.2 Various steps in computer language processing

You probably identify the steps in a compiler shown in Figure 9.2 as the various steps of speech processing as shown in Figure 9.1. The code generator in a compiler is the equivalent of extracting the meaning of the conveyed information through the speech.

I have also shown several memory blocks that are used by the complier during the processing. Some of these blocks are

- Pre-stored information such as pre-defined language specific 'keywords', the grammar rules for the language and the machine description such as instruction set, register architecture and other processor details.

- Symbol table that keeps track of symbols – variables, procedure names etc., syntactical arrangement of the words in the input description, and an intermediate representation of the code. These memory blocks are built as and when the processing is done and discarded once the processing is completed. So they are temporary working memories.

Speech processing involves different memory accesses

Every language has several predefined words that are part of the language: for example, the conjuncts that are used to connect words in a sentence. Also, there are predefined grammar rules that are used for syntax analysis. A database of pre-defined information about various real life objects is also utilized while performing semantic analysis, and inferring implied meaning. All these information are stored in various memories that need to be accessed while processing the incoming speech.

As the information is processed, the brain may also use several intermediate results that were temporarily created. These could be phrases or qualifiers that are nested within the sentence. All these temporarily created information are held in working memory till the processing is completed.

In a larger context, understanding of speech is not restricted to understanding individual sentences. They involve inferring the meaning in a given context. That means the processing may have to access whole lot of previously stored information relating to the subject be ing talked about. So, different types of memory accesses are involved while processing speech.

Processing sentences with complex structure

A sentence with a complex structure with nested phrases needs elaborate mechanism to not only validate the sentence but also infer its meaning. For example, the sentence which we talked about earlier, namely, 'He ate the pie that was made by the old lady who lives in the house behind the bridge' needs complex processing and also intermediate storage The meaning of this sentence may be inferred in a hierarchical way as shown in Figure 9.3.

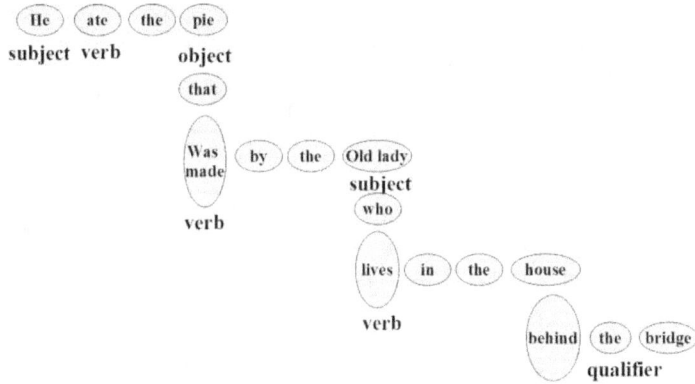

Figure 9.3 A sentence comprehension example

In general, the phrases in a given sentence can be nested arbitrarily deep making the processing difficult. Each phrase needs to be processed in turn, the result stored temporarily, and these results have to be finally combined to give the meaning of the sentence.

This kind of phrase wise processing of a complex sentence may take place by the combined action of more than one neural network, each trying to match a given phrase with a template. It is possible that a phrase might match more than one template and only one of the matches is valid in a given context. In such cases, the neural networks involved in processing them may compete with each other and only those who have maximum support from the context may win. Other interpretations die down.

As compared to this scenario, processing complex sentences in a computer may happen quite sequentially – from top to bottom, left to right.

Handling of nested structures by a computer (you may skip this if you choose to)

A compiler – a computer program that tries to understand another computer program written in a high level language - uses what is called a 'shift-reduce parser' to handle nested constructs.

This parser works by maintaining a stack of words or partial results as the processing progresses. Scanning the sentence from left to right, the parser goes on shifting a newly encountered word on to the stack. When the top part of the stack matches a grammar rule, that part of the stack is replaced by a temporary result. This is called reduction (see Figure 9.4 for a simplified view)

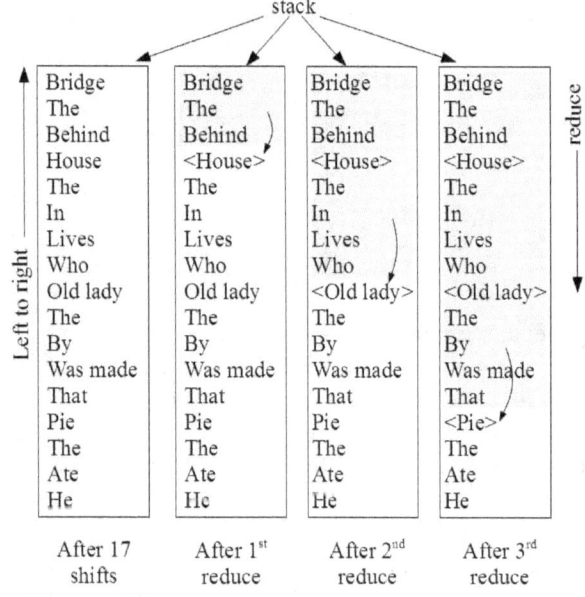

Figure 9.4 The way a shift-reduce parser would have processed the example sentence

This process of shifting and reducing continues till the end of the sentence is reached. Whatever remains on the stack at that time is reduced to arrive at the meaning of the sentence.

Compared to the brain, a computer works totally sequentially and the grammar it can handle is more or less unambiguous as well as context free.

How are language processing neural networks set up?

Though the exact working of these neural networks is not yet clear, scientists are figuring out the stages in which these neural networks are setup by studying how a child learns its native language.

No one learns his or her mother tongue by learning the grammar first. The grammar is gradually developed by repeated exposure to several instances of grammatically correct sentences that the child hears in its surrounding.

It seems that all human languages in the world have similar basic structure. All of them have sentences with a predefined grammar. Each sentence has noun, verb and other conjuncts. The exact form of these nouns, verbs, conjuncts and grammar rules may differ from language to language. Each language also has a way of emphasizing nouns or verbs. They have an order in which nouns and verbs appear in a sentence.

Scientists say that many of the networks needed for lexical processing are built as early as 28 weeks of gestation. While still in its mother's womb, the child listens to the conversations made outside (the body of its mother). Though it does not make any sense out of it, it helps in setting up and fine tuning necessary neural networks to match the nuances of the native language of the child. Post delivery, the child's brain refines these networks further and templates to match often occurring simple sentences get developed. For example – 'This is Mom', 'This is Dad' and so on.

Initially, the conjuncts are ignored and only the templates such as '<?> is <?>' are formed. The bold lettered words in these templates can be filled by various things. Repeated exposures to sentences with similar templates result in setting up higher level neural networks that try to generalize these sentence structures and infer grammatical rules. That is how grammar is gradually built, as if bootstrapped.

Having seen what is involved in processing of language, and how the necessary infrastructure for the processing is built, the next obvious question is 'in which part of the brain does this processing take place?'

Today we have sophisticated tools to monitor the activities of the brain. But long ago when no such tools were available, some scientists made some insightful observations that seem to be valid even to this day, well almost. These were the observations by two neurologists Broca and Wernicke, which have become the landmarks in the study of language processing in human beings.

Landmark observations of Broca and Wernicke

Way back in 1861, a neurologist namely Broca studied some patients who had lost their ability to speak after suffering a paralytic stroke. Broca found that some specific region in the left hemisphere of the brain in these patients was damaged.

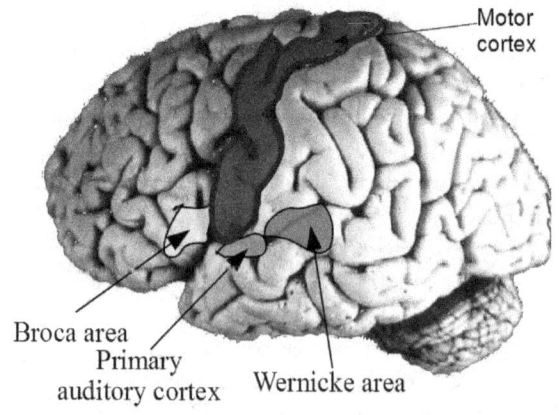

Figure 9.5 Broca and Wernicke areas of language processing (left hemisphere)

This made Broca conclude that this region is the place where speech production takes place.

Later in 1874 another neurologist Wernicke observed that there is another region in the brain, the damage to which caused language perception problems in the patients. This region was also in the left hemisphere of the brain. In due course, each of these regions came to be known after them as Broca area – responsible for speech production, and Wernicke area – responsible for speech perception.

This hemispheric asymmetry – only the left hemisphere for language processing – was taken for granted and continued to be propounded for almost a century till new tools to monitor brain activities emerged. But most text books of neuroscience and psychology still talk about these observations. For the last couple of decades new findings are surfacing, forcing the scientists to rethink on these old models.

Recent rethinking on original theories

Based on MRI and PET scans scientists have been able to question the century old theories on language processing and speech production in the brain. Various alternative theories have been proposed. The common observations of these theories seem to be the following.

- Broca and Wernicke areas are not the only two areas involved in speech production and speech perception. There are other areas in the brain as well.

- It is not true that speech perception is left brain dominated. The processing takes place in the right hemisphere as well. Each hemisphere handles different aspects of speech perception.

- As the input speech structure becomes more and more complex, several distant areas in the entire brain also get involved in the perception.

- Certain regions in the Broca area are also activated during speech perception and not just the Wernicke area.

- Just like in the case of visual processing, in language processing too there seem to be two paths – ventral stream and dorsal stream – along which the processing takes place. Ventral paths are involved in language perception – the "what" aspect, and the dorsal path is involved in language production – the "how" aspect. Some scientists even talk about multiple ventral paths.

Equipped with powerful tools like fMRI and PET, scientists have been able to identify various specific areas in the brain where different aspects of speech perception take place. Several theories have been proposed to explain the activation of Broca area during speech perception. What seems evident is that Broca and Wernicke areas are not as well defined and circumscribed as originally thought. There seem to be several structures in these areas that are shared by both speech perception, as well as speech production. Working memory could one typical candidate.

At the moment, most research seems to be hovering around identifying various structures utilized in language processing. More research is needed before we can clearly answer the "how" questions related to language processing.

10 How do we perform physical action?

For a primitive being, physical action may be restricted to catching its prey or defending itself from possible threats to its life. But physical action is so essential to us that we cannot spend even a moment without physical movements. Our speech, activities, sports, playing an instrument or even driving a motor car all involve complex physical movements. We probably cannot think of ourselves without some movement or the other.

How does the brain control all these physical movements? Not all aspects of this extremely complex function of our mind are fully understood. We do seem to have answers to "what" and "where" questions. The questions about "how" are yet to be answered. Let us start with simple intentional voluntary movements.

Effortful voluntary movements

Take for example we want to drink the mug of coffee kept on the table in front of us. Even this simple day-to-day act of ours involves quite a lot of complex issues that we seem to often take for granted.

Firstly, we need to have an idea of our body position with respect to the position of the mug placed on the table. Next, we need to make a series of movements that take our hand to the mug and finally to hold it using our fingers. Without our knowledge, our brain computes the force needed to lift the mug from the table. If the mug is full, we need to exert more force; and if it is not so full, less force.

Once the mug is grabbed and lifted, we need to make another series of movements to bring the mug to our lips so that we can sip the coffee in the mug. All along, the tilt of our hand, fingers and so on should be right so that coffee in the mug does not spill out. Also, the trajectory in which we move the mug should be such that it exactly reaches the lips and not the nose or some other facial part. Once we start sipping the coffee, we get the reward for doing all this action. All our actions were in anticipation of this reward.

What are we doing exactly? We are translating our intention to bring the cup to our lips into a series of fine joint movements – the joints in our shoulder, arm, wrist, and fingers. These movements have to be executed in a well defined sequence, at a well defined speed exerting the appropriate force at each stage. These movements are guided by our vision and our touch sense that continuously help in correcting wrong movements, if any.

All this looks quite simple and very routine. But the internal operation of this seemingly simple act is not that simple. Several systems in our body have to co-ordinate to make this happen. Let us start from the action end – various joint movements.

How are various joints moved?

Every joint in our body is attached to muscles called skeletal muscles. There are two types of muscles. *Joint flexor muscles* when activated make a joint close and a *joint extensor muscles* make the corresponding joint to open when activated. There are also other muscles that attach to soft tissues such as the muscles that move our eyes, tongue and so on.

Each muscle is made up of thousands of muscle fibers. Each of these muscle fibers is controlled by a special neuron called alpha motor neuron. Each such motor neuron controls one or more muscle fibers. The connectivity between these neurons and the muscles is provided through the spinal cord as shown in Figure 10.1.

Just to give an analogy, muscles are like the magnetic coils that move the pins in a print head of a printer, the spinal cord and the nerve fibers are like the electrical cable that connects your computer to the printer. The motor area of the brain plays the role of the CPU of your computer.

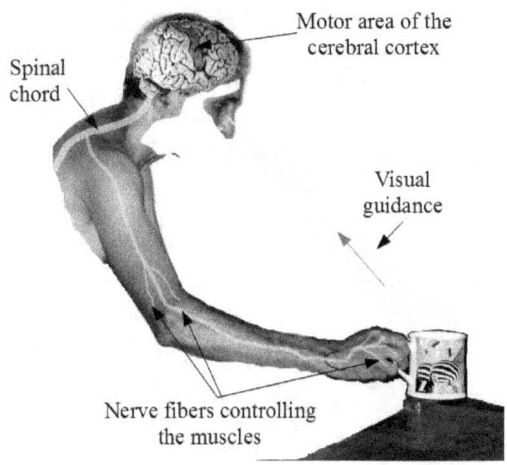

Figure 10.1 Simple voluntary act of lifting a coffee mug

A sequence of movement instructions flows from the brain, to appropriate muscles via the spinal cord and associated bundle of nerve fibers. But this is not a simple one way communication. There is backward flow of information, mainly guided by vision and touch sense, which continuously modulates the sequence of instructions, keeping track of the error in the movement.

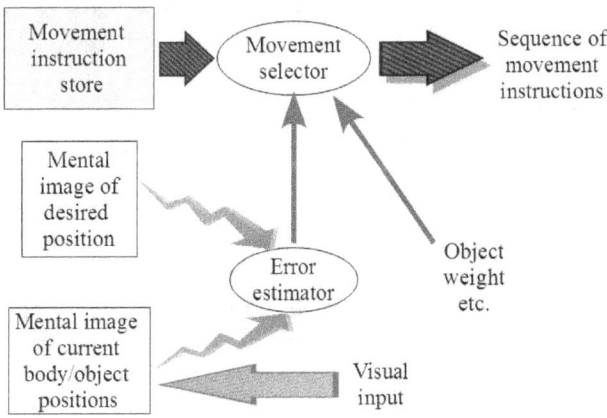

Figure 10.2 Instruction sequence generation in voluntary movement

There is also other information such as an estimate of the weight of the mug, level of coffee in the mug and so on, that are passed back. These feedbacks help in deciding the force to be applied in lifting the mug, the tilt to be made while drinking the coffee from the mug, and so on.

Most important of all, is that we need to pay attention to the act of moving the mug to our lips. Or else, we may spill the coffee on our dress!

This is how our voluntary movements take place. As compared to this, we make so many other movements that require almost no effort or attention. These are the movements or the skills that we have acquired as a result of prior learning. Let us see how these work.

Effortless skilled movements

During our lifetime, all of us acquire several skills – be it playing a musical instrument, driving a vehicle or operating a machine, or simply playing a game. Each of these has two phases – a learning phase and a post learning phase.

During the learning phase, our movements are effortful and need attention. We learn by making a series of movements repeatedly, fine tuning the movements at each repetition. The sequence of movements as well as the relative timings between these movements is refined till we achieve perfection.

There are several things that guide us in the process of learning. Firstly, in each cycle, the memory of past learning gives us a starting point from which we proceed to better our performance. At each cycle of learning, as in the previous case of voluntary movement, an error feedback and correction mechanism works continuously to refine the sequence of movements, both in terms of the individual movements as well as the timing between them. This error feedback could be visual or through a tutor who points out the error.

Also, a cost/reward estimator works to find out whether a specific movement increases the cost or reward. The cost could be the effort needed for the movement and the reward could be the gain due to a right movement. This cost/reward estimator also guides the movement selection. In addition, the reward mechanism also reinforces the previously stored procedural memory and refines it further to enjoy a better reward. These steps are summarized in Figure 10.3.

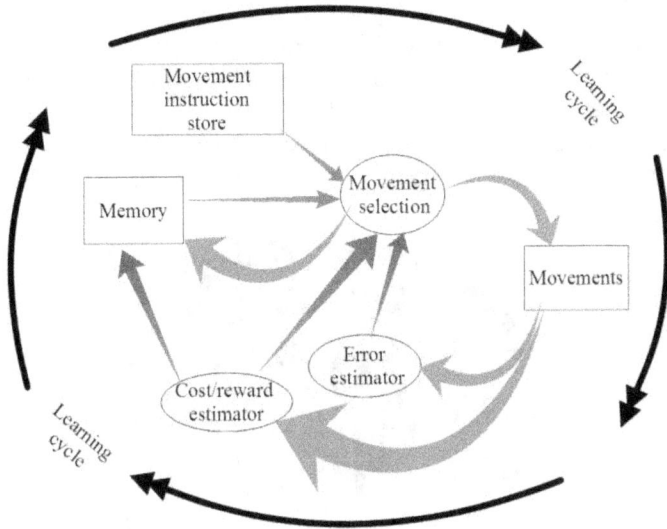

Figure 10.3 Skill learning cycle

In a series of learning cycles, we improve upon our movement skills and arrive at a perfect sequence of movements. Simultaneously, these sequences are continuously updated in the memory so that they can be used in future with minimal effort. Over a period of time these learned skills become almost automated requiring minimal attention, post learning.

Our current understanding of how various blocks in Figure 10.2 and Figure 10.3 are implemented is far from complete. We have some idea about where these functions may be taking place. There are some theories about how these are implemented. These theories as well as the roles of different parts of the brain in executing the movement are sometimes conflicting and are continuously refined as more clarity is reached. In the next sections, I will summarize our current understanding about the role of different brain regions in performing physical movements.

Motor cortex plays the major role

The motor region of the cerebral cortex plays an important role in our physical movements. This region has many areas that take part in different aspects of physical motion. Some of these areas are connected with other regions of the cerebral cortex either to receive visual inputs, or to get inputs about the motivation for the movement.

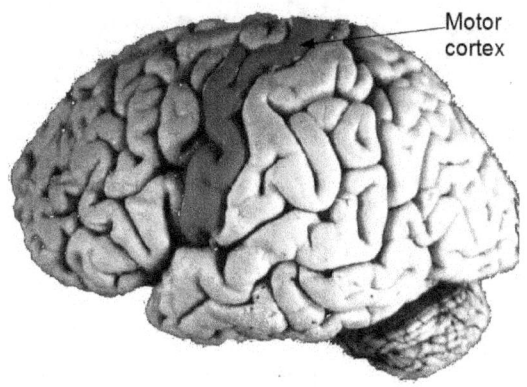

Motor cortex

Figure 10.4 Motor cortex that plays a predominant role in movement

There are connections to the spinal cord through which the movement instructions are finally delivered. There are also connections to other important structures within the brain such as Basal ganglia and Cerebellum about which I will talk about in the next section.

The steps involved in initiating the movements

There are mainly two steps before a movement is initiated. Firstly a mental model of the movement is made based on the motivation for the movement, position of the target object, and the position of our body with respect to the target object. This mental model is quite abstract and general.

Once this model is made, this model is translated into a series of actual 'movement prototypes'. These movement prototypes are groups of movement instructions that are specific to the task at hand. These prototypes are previously learnt and stored in the motor cortex as specialized neural networks. This learning occurs in the development stages of our brain and as we interact with objects of different shapes and sizes.

For example, if the target object is a cup, we probably use our thumb and the forefinger to hold the cup. If it is a mug then we use all four fingers except the thumb. In case the object is a glass, we shape our fingers in a cupping fashion to encircle the glass, and so on. Our exposure to newer and newer objects that we come across in our life builds more and more action prototypes.

These prototypes need to be sequenced one after another with appropriate delays in between so that there would be smooth movement of our hand and fingers.

The movement instructions in these prototypes are just tentative. Before they actually drive the respective muscles, they need to be specialized to suit the actual conditions. All mugs need not have identical size, nor are their weight and other properties identical. So depending on the actual condition, some of the instructions in these prototypes have to be further refined.

Other issues associated with movements

As I said earlier, a voluntary action needs our attention. Thalamus is the brain structure involved in focusing our attention. The motor region has connections to thalamus as well. Further, in the case of learning a movement skill, this new skill has to be embedded in the motor cortex for future usage. The brain achieves this by setting up new neural networks through the process of synaptic plasticity.

The implication of the movement also has to be stored in the memory for future reference. That means the brain has to establish associations between this action and related information in the memory that is previously stored.

There are two structures namely the Basal ganglia and Cerebellum that coordinate with the motor cortex in achieving all this. Let us briefly look at these structures and discuss their roles.

Basal ganglia and Cerebellum play important supporting roles

Basal ganglia and Cerebellum are important for smooth execution of movements and for learning new motor skills. Figure 10.5 shows these structures along with other related structures in the brain.

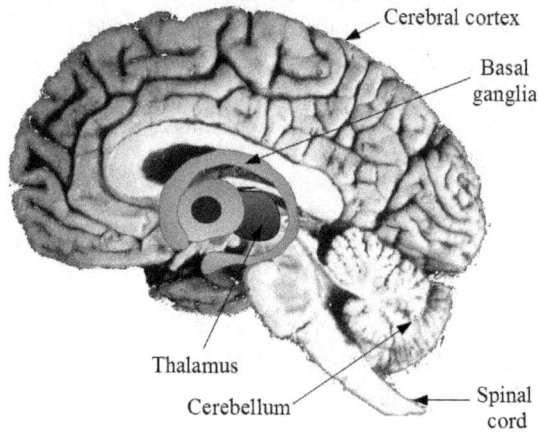

Figure 10.5 Basal ganglia and Cerebellum (sectional view)

Let us now briefly look at the roles of these two structures in coordinating physical movements in conjunction with the motor cortex.

Role of Basal ganglia

Basal ganglia are a group of neural structures that have various roles apart from their role in movement co-ordination. Despite decades of intense study and volumes of experimental results, the exact role of Basal ganglia is still widely debated. Different studies have come up with different hypotheses. Among these, the following are some noteworthy theories.

1. Basal ganglia are involved in selection of movement instructions and suppression of potentially competing actions and reflexes. Though this was what originally theorized, recent studies seem to indicate that this is not true. Basal Ganglia may not have any role in movement selection or inhibition.

2. They are involved in the control of scale of movement and related cost/reward functions. How fast or slow a movement is made decides the benefits/loss due to such movement. Basal ganglia are believed to provide an estimate of the rewards/costs involved in 'movement gain'. This theory seems to be valid.

3. They may be playing a crucial role in online correction of movement errors. As and when a movement is made, there is a need to provide feedback on possible 107s and correct the movement to reduce the errors in real time. Recent studies seem to suggest that the Basal ganglia are not involved in such error correction, though some earlier theories attributed such a role to Basal ganglia.

4. Basal ganglia aide in leaning of skills and their retention and recall. This seems to be the most important function of the Basal ganglia. With the help of special neuro-chemical called Dopamine, Basal ganglia are believed to provide quick reinforcement of synaptic connections between neurons in various neural networks in early phases of learning a motor skill. This reinforcement helps the Hebbian learning as we discussed in Chapter 5

   However, this learning and associated synaptic plasticity is only the initial stage. The long term retention of the learnt skill takes place in the cerebral cortex and not in Basal Ganglia as earlier thought. Recent studies indicate that Basal Ganglia do not retain the skill or execute them on recall later.

Role of cerebellum

The cerebellum is supposed to play important roles in the exertion of appropriate force and in fine tuning the timing between movements.

While gripping or holding an object the force applied should be optimum. Motor cortex cannot do this based on sensory information since the real time sensory processing to get the feedback involves delays of the order of 100 milliseconds. The action cannot be delayed for that long. Instead, cerebellum tries to predict the consequences of the action and use this prediction to decide the required force even before the movement is made.

The force needs to be exerted not only while gripping an object, but also while moving an object against the force of gravity. Cerebellum uses its predictive machinery to exert appropriate forces.

The cerebellum is also supposed to play an important role in timing of movements. Movement of a limb to reach an object is not as simple as it seems. A set of muscles, often called *agonist muscles*, try to move the limb forward, and another set of muscles, often called *antagonist muscles*, try to restrict the forward movement.

Left alone, the agonist muscles could overshoot the target, moving the limb beyond the intended object. This is prevented by the antagonist muscles that apply a break, sort of. The timing between the activation of the agonist muscles and the antagonist muscles is very important for a smooth movement of the limb. This timing is supposedly controlled by the cerebellum.

Timing is also crucial when we move a limb rapidly, say while throwing a ball. The speed with which different parts of the arm move decides the velocity with which the ball leaves the hand and hits the target.

Cerebellum's role as a timer

Initially it was thought that cerebellum acts like a timer with a fixed clock period, something like the clock in a computer. But these ideas have changed now. The current understanding is that cerebellum acts like a timer that uses variable relative timings, relative with respect to states of different muscles involved in the movement. The same set of movements can be performed slowly or fast depending on the need, or the skill acquired. The timings between sub-movements changes relative to each other and not in the absolute sense.

So effectively, the motor cortex in coordination with Basal Ganglia and the Cerebellum enable us to perform various movements. Many regions of our brain also provide information to these structures in that role.

11 Our emotions, beliefs and free will

After discussing several 'objective' aspects of our mind, I will now touch upon some of the other aspects of our mind that are generally considered to be 'subjective' and beyond objective investigation.

All of us undergo various emotions. We have our own set of beliefs and of course we have our own 'free will'. These are the things that make us different from inanimate things. All the same, these are the aspects that are difficult to clearly define.

Science does not accept anything that is purely subjective. It does not accept any non material entity like soul. It views our mind as just the brain in action or at most something that emerges as a result of the functioning of the brain. Since the mind is a material entity, whatever that emerges from it has to be material in nature and should be amenable to investigation in the same way as any other material entity – this is what science firmly believes in. (see my book – *"Important missing dimensions in our current understanding of the Mind - Marvels of the Mind Part II"* for an alternate view)

In this chapter, I will go with the current scientific view and discuss the way our current science goes about investigating these supposedly subjective aspects of our mind in a purely objective way. The conclusions arrived at are not only not undisputed, but could potentially make most of us uncomfortable. Let us look at them one by one.

Our emotions have a neural basis

Scientists have been looking for neural correlates of emotions – the neural mechanisms in the brain that correspond to our emotions. Several experiments involving various emotions have been conducted to see which regions of the brain act to produce the effect that we refer to as emotions.

The most prominent among these emotions are the maternal love of a mother to her children and the romantic feelings of a person to his/her mate. These emotions are often eulogized and considered to be the finest of human emotions. These are also the emotions essential for the most basic aspect of evolution, namely procreation and upkeep of the progeny.

Can a mother's love for her child be just a result of some activity in the neural networks in her brain? Can a lover's dedication and bonding for his/her mate be just another set of neurons working together? It is difficult to believe them to be so. But scientists say that it is just that.

Origins of maternal and romantic love

Scientists undertook detailed studies to investigate the happenings in our brain when someone undergoes maternal love or romantic love. A group of volunteers were subjected to these emotions and their brain activities were recorded using functional MRI techniques. The results were interesting.

In one such experiment a group of mothers were asked to view the pictures of their kids as well as the pictures of some other kids, either known to them or totally strangers. Scientists observed that when these mothers viewed the pictures of their kids, distinct areas of their brain are activated correlating with the emotion they experienced while they thought about their own beloved children. But not all these areas were activated when they viewed the pictures of other kids.

Similarly, when pictures of one's mate were shown, the regions of the brain that got activated were different from those when the person was viewing the picture of some acquaintance or a stranger.

Scientists have identified two neuro-hormones *vasopressin* and *oxytocin* that are involved in the formation and maintenance of attachment between individuals. Several studies on rodents and primates have confirmed that there exists a tight coupling between attachment processes and the neural systems for reward. These hormones activate the 'reward centers' in the brain, motivating the related activity.

Interestingly, the same neuro-hormones are involved in the attachment between mother and child (and vice versa) and in the long-term romantic bonding between adults. However, the exact brain regions that respond to these hormones may differ to some extent depending on the type of love – parental or romantic. By and large, they activate almost similar areas. This is probably obvious given the fact that both are evolutionary mechanisms involved in procreation and upbringing of the progeny.

Scientists have confirmed the roles of these regions by artificially suppressing their activity through pharmacological methods (using different drugs). For example, rats in which corresponding regions were suppressed showed no maternal love for their young ones, which would have been there otherwise.

What is further interesting is that along with the activation of some reward regions, some other regions that are normally involved in negative judgment are deactivated during these emotions. So a person in 'love' - whether maternal or romantic, tends to ignore the shortcomings of the beloved.

Further interesting observation was that the regions that are involved in making judgments about social reaction are also suppressed. So, these emotions work with a dual mechanism of 'reward for the emotion' and 'ignore the consequences'. Probably that is what makes 'love' blind!

Let us move on to the next topic namely our beliefs.

Can our beliefs do miracles?

I know of an Indian Swami who claims that he can cure any disease purely by his will power. If you go to him with any health problem, the Swami just closes his eyes, meditates for a while, and waves his hand as if he is driving away your illness. And lo! Your illness is gone. At least that is what the Swami claims. This Swami with impressive academic credentials shows meticulously kept records of the cases he has cured. He even challenges anyone to prove him wrong.

We keep coming across books where the authors claim that they have a *mantra* that can do anything. You want to 'remote control' your lover? or you want to win a poker game? All this can be done just by chanting a mantra for a few seconds!

There are certain medical systems (I wouldn't mention their name since they are highly popular) that have neither scientifically approved basis, nor support from large scale empirical studies. Yet these systems have a long line of adherents who can vouch for their efficacy.

In southern states of India you can see devotees in some Hindu temples who stab their bodies with sharp objects or hang themselves through chains attached to hooks pierced into their backs! They even walk on burning embers bare footed! None of these seem to cause them any pain!

The promoters of all the phenomena that I have mentioned above give various explanations to support their claims – Psychic power, cosmic power, strange yet to be discovered science, God and so on.

Science does not as yet approve of any of these. Definitely in a book discussing scientific findings I am not going to talk about these aspects. But yes, there is a strong undercurrent of belief in all these. Can our beliefs really do miracles?

Probably we cannot generalize. But definitely in some cases our beliefs can do miracles and we have scientific explanations about how they work. In this section, I am going to talk about these.

Beliefs can change the functioning of our minds

Scientists have long known that our beliefs can help us in reducing our physical pain. Or in other words, they can work like an analgesic. Just a powerful suggestion from someone we have faith, or even some fake treatment from a witch doctor can rid us from most pains. Scientists call this as placebo effect.

What is a placebo effect?

The placebo effect is an effect caused by our beliefs and values, which shapes our brain processes related to perception and emotion and, ultimately, mental and physical health. Scientists have of late come to accept that "subjective" concepts, such as expectation and value, have identifiable physiological bases, and that these bases are powerful modulators of basic perceptual, motor, and internal processes. Lot of progress has been made recently in understanding the neural basis of these effects. Let us see some of these findings.

Beliefs can reduce pain

In the case of pain relief, scientists have confirmed that our brains can generate opium like chemicals when a person strongly believes that a certain act or fake medicine relieves him of pain. These chemicals have similar effect as opium on various brain centers that are responsive to such chemicals. So the person with strong belief and expectation from such a belief can rid of the pain even though no actual medication is given. The medicine is internally generated by the brain itself!

Scientists have confirmed this fact by administering the person with drugs that are known to mask the effect of opium. When such drugs are administered, the pain relief achieved through belief also gets masked and the patient feels the pain in spite of the belief. Belief does not cure the cause of pain but merely suppresses our awareness of that, like any analgesic would have done.

Beliefs can help some Parkinson's disease afflicted patients

Placebo effect has been seen to be effective in treating patients suffering from Parkinson's disease. These patients normally have difficulty in bodily movement. When such patients were given a powerful suggestion or administered a fake drug to make them believe that the drug would reduce their problems with physical movements, that therapy indeed helped some patients.

A neuro chemical called dopamine helps in our bodily movements. This chemical is normally produced in a brain structure called *striatum*. In patients suffering from Parkinson's disease, normally this chemical is not produced adequately. But scientists found that strong expectation driven by belief can stimulate this brain structure to produce dopamine and result in the improvement of bodily movements.

Scientists have studied how this effect works by monitoring the activities of the brain in such patients through electrodes planted in their brain. Normally, Parkinson's disease afflicted patients are implanted with electrodes in their brain for deep brain stimulation, as part of the regular treatment. Scientists used these electrodes to probe the effects of placebo.

Scientists have also observed that even the normal drug treatment for Parkinson's disease is more effective if it is fortified by a placebo.

Beliefs can even reduce chronic depression

Depression is one of the most debilitating conditions. Several remedies are available for treating chronic depression. Scientists have found that even placebo or expectations driven by strong belief can help in such cases.

Using fMRI and PET scans, scientists have studied the structural changes that take place in the brain when various treatments for depression are given. They found that even when placebo effect takes place, similar structural changes in the brain can be seen.

So, effectively a strong belief and expectation driven by the belief can help one in minimizing the effects of depression or at least aid in making the normal depression treatment more effective.

Beliefs could trigger other mechanisms

Apart from internal production of neuro chemicals, the placebo or strong belief can trigger other mechanisms in the brain.

- Beliefs can reduce the anxiety of the person regarding the problem. In many cases we feel the severity of the pain more, if we are in an anxious state. Our beliefs could reduce anxiety and hence reduce the pain indirectly.

- Beliefs can also divert our attention from the problem. Many a times, we undergo a minor injury but we will not even be aware of it. Only when our attention is drawn towards it by a swelling or bleeding, we feel the pain. Placebo may be diverting our attention and helping us in reducing our problem.

- Our brain generally makes an estimate about how harmful an event is. This is called threat perception. If the threat perception is not significant, our brain may simply ignore the event and we would not even know about it. Strong belief could suppress regions in the brain that are involved in computing threat perception.

A word of caution

Before one can jump to the conclusion that our beliefs can do miracles and it is proven scientifically, one should keep the following in mind.

- Firstly, not all people are 'placebo responsive'. That is, belief does not work for everyone. It depends on the vulnerability of the person and prior conditioning.

- Secondly, placebo's only help us in managing the problems and not solving the problems. More so if the problem is caused by an external event. We can prevent ourselves from getting wet by holding an umbrella, but we cannot stop the rain.

• Thirdly, our beliefs may help us in overcoming problems in which we are involved. Changing some event totally outside ourselves or solving someone else's problem is something that probably needs more than belief.

After emotion and belief there is one more aspect that makes each one of so 'animate'. That is our 'free will'. Let us next see how science views this free will.

The so called 'free will' originates from the brain?

I have put a question mark after the heading above, to indicate that the scientists have not yet undisputedly confirmed that our so called free will is not 'free' after all.

Most events in our world are driven by a specific cause. An effect does not take place unless there is a cause. A fan for example, starts rotating only when the switch is turned on; it changes its speed only when the regulator is turned, and so on. An inanimate thing never does anything on its own. Or in other words, it has no 'free will'. As against this, an animate thing like we ourselves, have a 'free will'. We consider ourselves to be different since we can do things out of our own free will without driven by any cause.

But this assumption of ours was questioned by some neuro-physiological experiments performed by Benjamin Libet and his collaborators way back in 1980s. Many scientists have interpreted the outcome of these experiments as the confirmation that there is no such thing as 'free will'.

All our actions, including those we consider as based on our free volition are actually initiated by our brain even before we are aware of them! Or in other words, nothing – not even us – is beyond causality! – This is the view of some scientists, based on Libet's experiments.

What exactly did Libet do?

It was known since early 1960s that before we make any movement of our limbs, the motor cortex in our brain gets activated, as seen by slow build up of an electrical potential. This potential, measured from outside the skull at a region corresponding to the motor cortex was called 'readiness potential' or RP. This potential indicated that our motor cortex was getting ready to make the move.

Libet performed some experiments in which volunteers were asked to move their fingers as and when felt like moving. The important thing was that they have to record the exact time when they took the decision to move their finger and the time when they actually moved their fingers. Appropriate mechanisms were provided to help them in recording these events. These volunteers were also asked not to ponder over, before deciding to make the move, but to make the decision as spontaneously as possible.

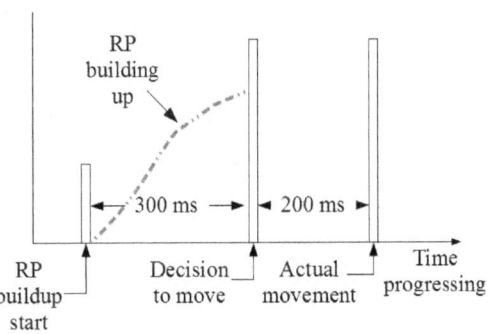

Figure 11.11 Libet's observations

Libet recorded the time when this RP started building up relative to the time at which the volunteers actually moved the fingers. He was surprised to find that even though the fingers moved some 200 milliseconds after the person decided to move the finger, RP buildup started more than 500 milliseconds before the actual movement. That means, the brain was getting ready to make the movement around 300 milliseconds even before the person decided to make the move!

How was Libet's observation interpreted by most scientists?

On the face of it, it was clear that the person's decision to make the movement was not voluntary after all. It was driven by the activity that was taking place in his brain even before he made a decision to make the movement. That means the assumed 'free will' was driven by a cause namely the prior activity in the brain. So it cannot be free.

Libet's experiment became highly controversial with rival groups giving opposing interpretations to the same findings. Added to this confusion, Libet himself pointed out that even though RP buildup started much before the decision, the actual movement always took place only after the decision. That means that the movement was actually initiated by the decision. This sparked further controversy as to what Libet was trying to imply. Some scientists even read 'neuro theology' in Libet's words and criticized him for that.

What seems to be generally accepted is that there is no 'free' agent (like soul, consciousness etc.) that takes decisions without a cause, as generally accepted. Whatever happens is driven by a cause and that cause is either an external event or the brain itself. In other words, the so called mind is either the brain in action or the effect of the activities of the brain. There is no separate entity that governs the mind.

But many philosophers tend to disagree with this conclusion. They point out to various flaws in such conclusions and Libet's observations that could lead to such conclusions. And the controversy continues.

12 Our consciousness

After discussing supposedly subjective notions like emotions, beliefs and free will in the previous chapter, I will now touch upon another notion that too has purely subjective connotations: that is our consciousness.

We often use the words consciousness and being conscious interchangeably as if they are synonymous. For us, being conscious either means the ability to respond to external events or to be aware of such events.

However, philosophers give a different meaning to this word. They emphasize more on how we experience events. They call it *phenomenal consciousness*. According to them, this is a purely subjective notion that is beyond objective description.

There is no way we can explain how we feel when we drink a good cup of coffee for example. That is some purely personal experience specific to us alone. The same cup of coffee may not give the same experience to another individual. Nor there is any way we can compare the two experiences.

As I said in the previous chapter, science does not believe in subjectivity. Our scientists insist on explaining everything in objective terms, including our experiences. There have been some attempts to explain the philosophic concept of consciousness objectively as some explainable function of the brain or the mind. These attempts though, appear contrived and not very convincing.

There are others who take a pragmatic view that there are more important aspects of the mind that are still not completely understood and our efforts need to be focused on them at the moment. I take the same stand and postpone the discussion on subjectivity to the next part of this book series namely – *"Important missing dimensions in our current understanding of the Mind - Marvels of the Mind Part II"*.

In this chapter, I will focus mainly on how the inputs to our experience are produced or how our mind works as a whole, aided by several semi-autonomous groups of functional units in the brain. The inputs to our experience and the experience itself may or may not be the same: something which I would not like to comment on here.

How do we get a conscious experience?

Our conscious experience is a result of various functional units in our brain working together in a coordinated manner. Though there is no centralized entity that orchestrates the activities of these almost independent functional units, our experience is as if the information produced by them is somehow combined together.

In earlier chapters, we have seen how different functional units of the brain work on various aspects of the functioning of our brain. Each of these functional units employs one or more neural networks to perform the task in hand. These neural networks are almost autonomous and work independently. Also, none of these have any idea of the global picture. Let me take a simple example to explain this.

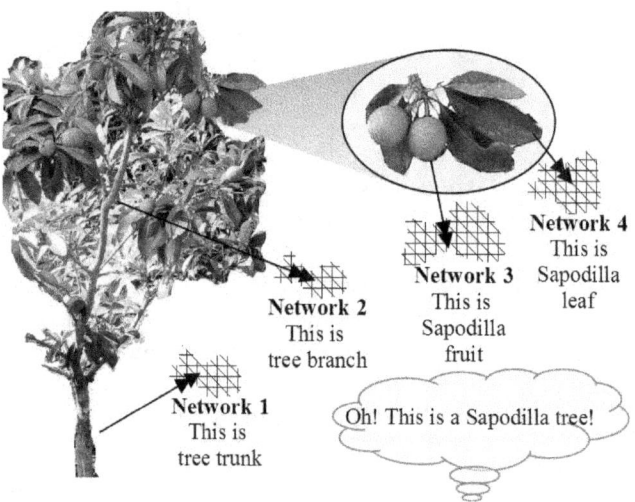

Figure 12.1 The problem of binding pieces of information

Look at the object that is shown in the left side of Figure 12.1. At once you recognize the object as a Sapodilla tree (assuming that you are familiar with the tree). This act of recognition is almost effortless and instantaneous. But do you realize the complexity of this simple function?

Several neural networks are involved in processing various aspects of this object. For simplicity, I have shown them as 4 neural networks: Network 1 to Network 4. Each of these networks operates independently – some may try to recognize the trunk of the tree, some the fruit and some other the leaf. None of them have the complete idea that it is various parts of a single object.

Each network may have its own complexity and may take its own time to process the information. Identifying the tree trunk may take less time than identifying the fruit as Sapodilla. Naturally, the outputs of these networks come at different times. Now the question is – how is it that we recognize the object as a Sapodilla tree and not as a collection of trunk, leaves, fruit and so on?

This is the so called *binding problem* that has confounded scientists for long. It is a problem about knowing how all these pieces of information from each network are 'bound' together into single combined information.

Various facets of the consciousness puzzle

Scientists observed that when all these networks are ready with information to be 'bound' together, all of them start firing in a synchronous fashion at their peak rates. They conjectured that this synchronous firing of networks working on different pieces of information 'somehow' encoded the combined information that we experience. But the scientists were not sure whether this synchronous firing was sufficient to create the combined information or whether it needed something else.

There were questions whether this combined information was assembled in some area of the brain so that it can be used for further processing or inducing experience. But no such region could be identified. Also it was not clear about what causes the synchronous firing.

There were other unanswered questions as well. In any perception task several lookups to pre-stored memory are needed. For example, in the example above, to identify what was being processed is a Sapodilla, needed matching with information stored in memory about Sapodilla. There could be several other brain resources that may have to be consulted before each network comes up with the results.

Once we have an experience, to be aware of the experience, this experience has to be recorded in our memory. We may even express our awareness of the experience through words or movements.

So the conscious experience involves coordination between various regions of the brain that may or may not be directly connected. They could be spread across entire brain. That being the case, how is it that each of these regions communicate with each other? Who connects them together and what coordinates exchange of information between these remote regions? This was the problem facing the scientists who were trying to explain the roots of our awareness.

Global workspace theory is a possible answer

Sometime in late 1980s Bernard Baars came up with a theory called *Global workspace theory* to explain how this complex interaction between various components of the brain takes place to give us a combined experience. He used a theatre metaphor to explain his theory.

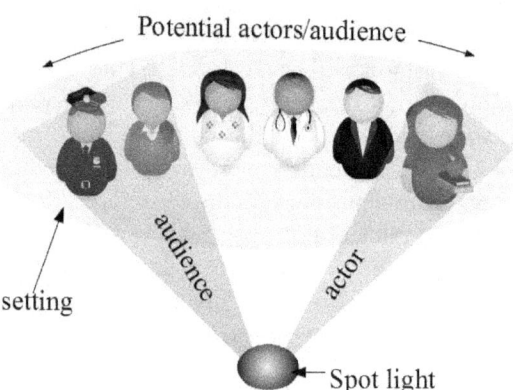

Figure 12.2 Bernard Baars' mind theatre

Potential actors/audience

setting

audience

actor

Spot light

He compared the brain to a theatre with audiences sitting and watching the play, and the actors who enact the play. The special feature of this theatre is that there is no fixed stage or gallery, but sometimes some audience become the actors and vice versa. A spot light focused on the actors and audience indicated who are currently active. The entire play takes place in the setting of pre stored context (i.e. our prior experiences).

Poetical imaginations apart, the Global workspace theory maps onto the following scenario. Our brain is the place where the action takes place. Different components of this mental drama are as follows.

1. A set of neural networks that produce information (actors in the metaphor)
2. A set of neural networks that receive this information (audience in the metaphor)
3. A mental context in which the processing takes place (the setting in the metaphor)
4. An attention mechanism (the spot light in the metaphor)
5. A mechanism to support the interaction between them. (audio system in the metaphor)

Viewed from the functional level, the actor/audience could be sense input processors, speech production networks, motor region, memory, thoughts, various evaluators and so on. These disjoint functional units are dynamically connected among themselves, as needed, through a network of connections setup by the attention system.

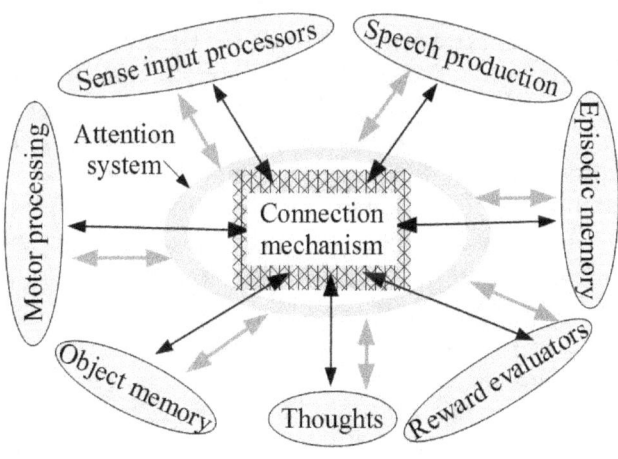

Figure 12.3 Global workspace setup

The attention system does the following

1. Selects the functional units to be connected
2. Enhances the activities in these chosen units
3. Sets up the connections between them appropriately

The entire arrangement could be as shown in Figure 12.3 above.

Either the attention selects the functional units that interact through the connection mechanism or alternatively, various functional units compete among themselves for the attention of the attention system and whoever wins in this competition succeeds in getting into the final setup. In terms of the theatre metaphor they will either become the actors or audience depending on who produces the information and who receives it. Others will either gradually become inactive or wait for their turn in the next act.

If you are familiar with computer system architecture, you may recognize the similarities between global workspace setup and a computer system.

A computer system analogy (you can skip this)

A computer system typically has a CPU, one or more I/O systems and memory. These almost autonomous entities are interfaced through what is called a *system bus*. Whenever two (or more) of these entities need to exchange information – one of them producing the information and the other consuming it – they get dynamically connected through the system bus.

The normal protocol is as follows.

1. Each entity that wants to get connected through the bus makes a *bus request*.
2. A *bus controller* arbitrates between various entities that may simultaneously raise a request based on pre-set *priority* and *grants* the bus to the entities that win the *arbitration*.
3. The entities that were off the bus (*tri-stated*) earlier and whose requests are granted now get connected to the bus. Others remain off the bus waiting for their request to be approved.
4. The connected entities exchange the information using the bus through which they are connected.

5. As seen from the bus, there would be high activity of information movement either way.

6. Once the entities finish their information exchange, they *release* the bus, allowing others to use the bus.

7. This process continues.

Figure 12.4 summarizes this setup between various subsystems of a computer.

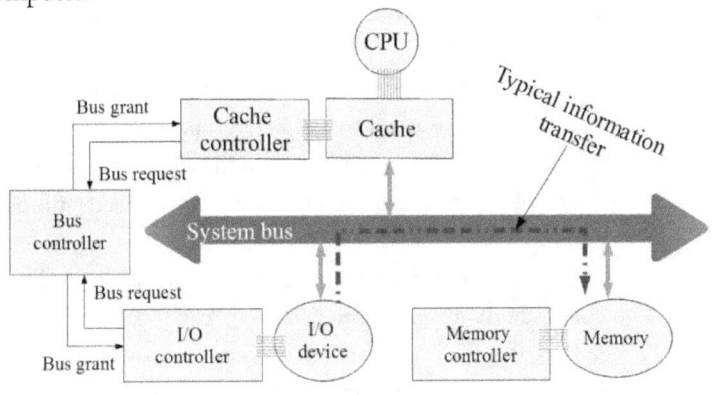

Figure 12.4 Computer system architecture

Some scientists term the process involving competition, selection and succeeding of the fittest in a global workspace as *Neural Darwinism*, striking an analogy with the Darwin's theory of biological evolution.

A couple of things can be noted in the arrangement shown in Figure 12.3

1. Unless we pay attention, information that needs interaction between multiple functional units in the brain, escapes our awareness.

   Often, we get a vague feeling that a person we don't remember having met earlier appears to be familiar. What could have happened is that we had seen the person earlier but had not paid attention to it. So his face was not registered in our conscious awareness. But it could well have been registered in some networks that processed the face even without our attention. That is why the face looks familiar, but we are not aware of having seen it earlier. If we had paid attention, that information would have moved from visual processing networks to our memory and we would have remembered having seen that person.

2. Our being aware is also needed for performing any complex set of movements unless it has become ingrained as a habit or skill.

   For example, while we are in the process of learning how to drive a car, we need to be fully conscious and pay attention. But once we mastered that skill, we almost don't need to pay any attention. The act of driving proceeds almost on its own.

3. Once a set of functional units are chosen for interaction, only one set of information exchange can take place. Others need to wait till the current exchange is over; the current connections are dismantled, and new connections are made.

   This means that our conscious experiences and acts are strictly sequential – one at a time. This is in contrast to the normal functioning of the brain where different functional units work in parallel and simultaneously.

   However, it is not clear whether this view is right, since we often see that we can do multiple tasks at a time. We can read this book and simultaneously listen to some music as well.

   Probably, the attention is rapidly switched between the two tasks, so fast that we feel that we are doing multitasking. This is like a multi-tasking computer operating system that keeps switching between multiple tasks giving the impression that the tasks are performed simultaneously.

   Alternatively, it is also possible that there are multiple interconnection mechanisms in the brain. As long as there is no conflict between shared resources, multiple interactions can go on simultaneously.

4. When we are engrossed in thoughts, we cannot perform any other activity. Similarly, when we are intensely involved in some action or perception, no thoughts cross our mind.

I have shown thoughts as one of the potential contenders to the global workspace usage. Thoughts are sporadically generated neural activities that produce almost the same kind of information as that produced by different functional units that process sense inputs.

The consequence of thoughts contending for the global workspace is that we can either think or act – strictly one at a time. But again, rapid switching of the attention may give us the impression of doing both together!

Assuming that the Global workspace theory is a valid explanation of how we consciously experience or act based on inputs that are received from different neural networks across the brain, the next question would be – how is this workspace implemented in the brain? This is what we will be seeing in the next section.

Brain structures that implement Global workspace

The structures we are looking for are the functional units that use the global workspace setup, the attention system, and the interconnecting mechanism. Some of the possible candidates are the following.

Users of the Global workspace: In the previous chapters we have seen various functional units spread all over the cerebral cortex that can potentially produce or consume information.

These could be vision processing networks, audio processing networks, speech processing networks, speech production networks, neural networks that implement motor functions, various types of memories, different networks that evaluate reward/cost, and so on. These are the ones that use the global workspace.

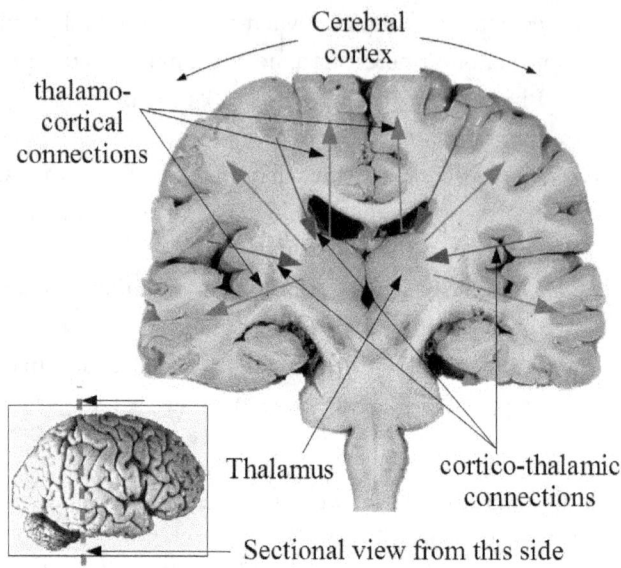

Figure 12.5 Global workspace implementation in the brain

<u>The attention mechanism:</u> It is well known that different parts of our brain can work even without our being aware. We are often aware of only a tiny bit of information that is produced in the brain. Most of the processing evades our consciousness. In other words, the brain processes are mostly subconscious. We will become aware of only those things that we need to be aware of and those we pay attention to.

It is generally observed that inactivating parts of the cerebral cortex, though affects some of the functionality, does not prevent us from being conscious of global events. Even if half the cerebral cortex is removed, we still remain conscious.

However, our consciousness gets totally switched off when some parts of a brain structure called thalamus is deactivated. That means that these structures in the thalamus are necessary for us to be conscious. They could be working as the attention system.

This view is further supported by the additional observation that thalamus has bidirectional connections – thalamo-cortical as well as cortico-thalamic - to almost the entire cerebral cortex as shown in Figure 12.5. These bidirectional connections can either aide in selecting the functional units, enhance their activities or could even help the functional units in drawing the attention of the attention system.

<u>The interconnection mechanism</u>: It is known that a large number of neurons called *inter neurons* are distributed throughout the cerebral cortex. These neurons may be playing the role of the interconnection mechanism between various functional units. These neurons may be relaying the information from one functional unit to another.

The attention sets up these inter neurons so that the appropriate connection is made. It is like the way our landline telephone exchanges connect caller and receiver lines. In cases needing long range connections, there could be a hierarchy of inter neurons just like the trunk exchanges in good old electro-mechanical telephone exchanges.

With this set of functional units, the attention system and the dynamically connected inter-neurons, we seem to be getting our conscious experiences as a phenomenon happening across the whole brain.

Epilogue

What you have read in the previous chapters is the result of the efforts to understand the working of the mind, by a variety of researchers from diverse fields, for the past 150 years of scientific research. This effort has been greatly made vigorous for the past few decades, thanks to the invention of several modern equipments and of course, the computers.

However, as you have probably noticed, we are still far from completely understanding the mind. There are several blanks to be filled in, several details to be explored into.

But there is one more face to this task. Science's insistence on objectivity seems to be a stumbling block that is preventing us from exploring the mind in all its dimensions. There are several simple common sense questions science fails to answer.

The fundamental question is – "Are we just a bundle of cells and neurons?" Even if this were true, the question "what is the purpose of this elaborate mechanism called mind?" faces us. The question the Sānkhya philosophers from ancient India put long back namely, "How can there be an instrument (the Sānkhya philosophers consider the mind as an instrument) without a user?" begs an answer. The simple scientific answer that it is just a consequence of biological evolution fails to convince.

Our scientific understanding tries to convince us that our emotions are just produced in the mind or the brain but there is actually none who experiences these emotions. Consciousness is just the 'awareness' without there being anyone who is 'aware of'. But it is our day to day experience that it is "we" who experience them.

To deliver a final blow on subjectivity, scientists even go to the extent of saying that the so called 'free will' does not exist and it is all in the brain!

All these efforts of science are aimed at evading the tricky issue of acceptance of any non material entity. Science insists that everything is material and can be examined, studied and understood solely using our senses. Anything that is beyond our sense perception – directly or indirectly - does not exist!

But there are other studies, also conducted by reputed scientists, which almost indicate that it is possible for a person to continue even after death by taking rebirth. According to these scientists a fair amount of personality traits get transferred from one existence to another.

Unless we rubbish these studies as fraudulent or errors in perception how do we explain transfer of information from one birth to another? It cannot be through the brain since the brain perishes with the body that dies.

Does this not imply that there can be something non material in to which some of the information in our brain can get transferred? And it is this non material stuff that actually gets transferred from one birth to another? It is not necessary that this non material thing has to be the soul. For example, ancient Buddhists, who did not accept the concept of soul, suggested their own mechanisms for this transfer without resorting to the concept of soul.

There are other dimensions as well. Our over reliance on our senses has limited us to the perceptible world we live in. But many great Yogis have endorsed the fact that there are states beyond what our senses and our minds can perceive! Are these just illusions? How sure are we that the world we perceive through our senses and the mind is really what it appears to be?

That brings us to the question of what is reality. Is reality defined by our sense perceptions? Are the worlds we live in, and that a bat lives in, different just because we have different types of senses?

All these questions point to the fact that there could be other aspects of the mind, science is yet to be aware of. In order to understand these other dimensions of our existence, science itself may need to undergo drastic changes in its outlook.

Interestingly, ancient philosophers had pondered over these points and had definite answers to these questions. I am not advocating their view points. But in the true spirit of science it may pay to keep an open mind and see whether we can learn anything from these ancient philosophies.

That is what I am going to do in the next part of this series namely *"Important missing dimensions in our current understanding of the mind - Marvels of the Mind Part II"*. I will look forward to joining you then in an altogether different journey to understand the mind.

The Bibliography

1. *Visual cognition: a new look at the two-visual systems model.* **M. Jeannerod and P. Jacob.** 2004, Neuropsychologia.

2. *Ventral and dorsal pathways for language.* **Dorothee Saur et.al.** 46, November 2008, Proc. of National Academy of Sciences, Vol. 105.

3. *Two visual systems re-viewed.* **A.D. Milner and M.A. Goodale.** 2008, Neuropsychologia, Vol. 46.

4. *Two hierarchically organized neural systems for object information in human visual cortex.* **Christina S Konen and Sabine Kastner.** 2, FEBRUARY 2008, NATURE NEUROSCIENCE, Vol. 11.

5. *Towards a New Neurobiology of Language.* **David Poeppel, Karen Emmorey, Gregory Hickok, and Liina Pylkka¨nen.** 32, October 2012, The Journal of Neuroscience, Vol. 41.

6. *Towards a cognitive neuroscience of consciousness: basic evidence and a workspace framework.* **Stanislas Dehaene and Lionel Naccache.** 2001, Cognition, Vol. 79.

7. *The Neuronal Basis of Long-Term Sensorimotor Learning.* **Yael Mandelblat-Cerf et.al.** 1, January 2011, The Journal of Neuroscience, Vol. 31.

8. *The Neural Mechanisms of Speech Comprehension: fMRI studies of Semantic Ambiguity.* **Jennifer M. Rodd, Matthew H. Davis and Ingrid S. Johnsrude.** August 2005, Cerebral Cortex, Vol. 15.

9. *The neural correlates of maternal and romantic love.* **Bartels, Andreas and Zeki, Semir.** 21, 2004, NeuroImage.

10. *The Molecular Biology of Memory Storage: A Dialog Between Genes and Synapses.* **Eric R. Kandel.** 5, October 2001, Bioscience Reports, Vol. 21.

11. *The Libet experiment and its implications for conscious will.* **Peter G.H. Clarke.** s.l. : The Faraday Institute for Science and Religion, February 2013.

12. *The Impact of Partial Phonological Contrast on Speech Perception.* **Elizabeth Hume and Keith Johnson.** 2003. Proceedings of the 15th International Congress of Phonetic Sciences.

13. **Kalanit Grill-Spector.** The functional organization of the ventral visual pathway and its relationship to object recognition. *FUNCTIONAL NEUROIMAGING OF VISUAL COGNITION.* 2003.

14. *The functional neuroanatomy of prelexical processing in speech perception.* **Sophie K. Scott and Richard J.S. Wise.** 2004, Cognition, Vol. 92.

15. *The Functional Neuroanatomy of Language.* **Gregory Hickok.** 6, September 2009, Phys Life Rev., Vol. 3.

16. **Robert Shapley, Michael Hawken and Dajun Xing.** The dynamics of visual responses in the primary visual cortex. *Progress in Brain Research,.* 2007, Vol. 165.

17. *The cortical organization of speech processing.* **Gregory Hickok and David Poeppel.** May 2007, NEUROSCIENCE, Vol. 8.

18. *The cortical language circuit: from auditory perception to sentence comprehension.* **Angela D. Friederici.** 5, May 2012, Trends in Cognitive Sciences, Vol. 16.

19. *The conscious access hypothesis : origins and recent evidence.* **Bernard J. Baars.** 1, 2002, Trends in Cognitive Science, Vol. 9.

20. *The Binding Problem.* **Holcombe.** 2009, The Sage Encyclopedia of Perception.

21. —. **Adina L. Roskies.** September 1999, Neuron, Vol. 24.

22. *The Basal Ganglia and Motor Control.* **Henk J. Groenewegen.** 2003, NEURAL PLASTICITY, Vol. 10.

23. *Task-Related Interaction between Basal Ganglia and Cortical Dopamine Release.* **Gae"tan Garraux et.al.** 27, December 2007, The Journal of Neuroscience, Vol. 52.

24. *Synaptic Mechanisms for Plasticity in Neocortex .* **Daniel E. Feldman.** 2009, Annu Rev Neurosci., Vol. 32.

25. *Speech perception: Some new directions in research and theory.* **David B. Pisoni.** July 1985, J Acoust Soc Am.

26. *Speech Perception, Word Recognition and the Structure of the Lexicon.* **David B. Pisoni, Howard C. Nusbaum, Paul A. Luce, and Louisa M. Slowiaczek.** August 1985, Speech Commun.

27. *Speech perception at the interface of neurobiology and linguistics.* **David Poeppel, William J. Idsardi and Virginie van Wassenhove.** 2008, Phil. Trans. R. Soc., Vol. 363.

28. *Speech perception as pattern recognition.* **Terrance M. Nearey.** 101, June 1997, J. of Acoustical Society of America, Vol. 6.

29. *Speech Perception as a Window for Understanding Plasticity and Commitment in Language Systems of the Brain.* **Janet F. Werker and Richard C. Tees.** November 2004, Wiley InterScience.

30. *Speech Perception and Language Acquisition in the First Year of Life.* **Judit Gervain and Jacques Mehler.** 2010, The Annual Review of Psychology, Vol. 61.

31. *Somatosensory Plasticity and Motor Learning.* **David J. Ostry et.al.** 15, April 2010, The Journal of Neuroscience, Vol. 30.

32. *Sleep and memory: a molecular perspective.* **Laurel Graves, Allan Pack and Ted Abel.** 4, April 2001, TRENDS in Neurosciences, Vol. 24.

33. *SEQUENTIAL ORGANIZATION OFMULTIPLE MOVEMENTS: Involvement of Cortical Motor Areas.* **Jun Tanji.** 2001, Annu. Rev. Neurosci., Vol. 24.

34. *Separate neural pathways for the visual analysis of object shape in perception and prehension.* **Melvyn A. Goodale et.al.** July 1994, Current Biology, Vol. 4.

35. *SELF: AN ADAPTIVE PRESSURE ARISING FROM SELF-ORGANIZATION, CHAOTIC DYNAMICS, AND NEURAL DARWINISM.* **ANGELA ALESSIA BRUZZO.** 4, 2007, Journal of Integrative Neuroscience, Vol. 6.

36. *Role of the Cerebellar Cortex in Conditioned Goal-Directed Behavior.* **Eric Burguie`re et.al.** 40, October 2010, The Journal of Neuroscience, Vol. 30.

37. *Role of Individual Basal Ganglia Nuclei in Force Amplitude Generation.* **Matthew B. Spraker et.al.** 2, August 2007, J Neurophysiol., Vol. 98.

38. *Rethinking the neurological basis of language.* **Laurie A. Stowe, Marco Haverkort and Frans Zwarts.** 2005, Lingua, Vol. 115.

39. *Reorganization and plasticity in the adult brain during learning of motor skills.* **Julien Doyon and Habib Benali.** 2005, Current Opinion in Neurobiology, Vol. 15.

40. **Joe Z. Tsien.** Real-time neural coding of memory. *Progress in Brain Research.* 2007, Vol. 165.

41. *Paying attention to consciousness.* **John G. Taylor.** 5, May 2002, Trends in Congnitive Science, Vol. 6.

42. *Neuroscience: Toward Unbinding the Binding Problem.* **David Whitney.** 8, 2009, Current Biology, Vol. 19.

43. *Neuronal Avalanches in Neocortical Circuits.* **John M. Beggs and Dietmar Plenz.** December 2003, The Journal of Neuroscience,.

44. *Neuro-cognitive mechanisms of conscious and unconscious visual perception: From a plethora of phenomena to general principles.* **Markus Kiefer, Ulrich Ansorge, John-Dylan Haynes, Fred Hamker, Uwe Mattler, Rolf Verleger, and Michael Niedeggen.** 2007, Advances in Cognitive Psychology, Vol. 7 (Special issue).

45. *Neurobiological Mechanisms of the Placebo Effect.* **Fabrizio Benedetti, Helen S. Mayberg, Tor D. Wager, Christian S. Stohler, and Jon-Kar Zubieta.** November 2005, The Journal of Neuroscience.

46. *Neuroanatomical correlates of happiness, sadness, and disgust.* **Richard D. Lane et.al.** Juky 1997, The American Journal of Psychiatry.

47. *Neuroanatomical correlates of externally and internally generated emotion.* **Reiman, Eric M. et.al.** 1997, Am J. Psychiatry.

48. *Neural mechanisms of reward-related motor learning.* **Jeffery R Wickens, John N J Reynolds and Brian I Hyland.** 2003, Current Opinion in Neurobiology, Vol. 13.

49. *Neural Darwinism: Selection and Reentrant Signaling in Higher Brain Function.* **Gerald M. Edelman.** February 1993, Neuron, Vol. 10.

50. *Neural Darwinism and consciousness.* **Anil K. Seth, Bernard J. Baars.** 2005, Consciousness and Cognition, Vol. 14.

51. *Neural Correlates of Conscious Self-Regulation of Emotion.* **Mario Beauregard, Johanne Le´ vesque, and Pierre Bourgouin.** 2001, The Journal of Neuroscience, Vol. 21.

52. *Networks of Neurons, Networks of Genes: An Integrated View of Memory Consolidation.* **Teiko Miyashita, Stepan Kubik1,, Gail Lewandowski, and John F. Guzowski.** 3, March 2008, Neurobiol Learn Mem., Vol. 89.

53. *Molecular mechanisms of memory acquisition, consolidation and retrieval.* **Ted Abel and K Matthew Lattal.** 2001, Current Opinion in Neurobiology.

54. *Molecular and systems mechanisms of memory consolidation and storage.* **Huimin Wang, Yinghe Hu, Joe Z. Tsien.** 2006, Progress in Neurobiology, Vol. 79.

55. *MODELS OF THE CEREBELLUM AND MOTOR LEARNING.* **James C. Houk, Jay T. Buckingham and Andrew G. Barto.** 3, 1996, Behavioral and Brain Sciences, Vol. 19.

56. *Memory systems in the brain and localization of a memory.* **RICHARD F. THOMPSON AND JEANSOK J. KIM.** 1996. Proc. Natl. Acad. Sci. USA. Vol. 93.

57. *Memory consolidation and reconsolidation: what is the role of sleep?* **Robert Stickgold and Matthew P. Walker.** 8, August 2006, TRENDS in Neurosciences, Vol. 28.

58. *Making Sense of Semantic Ambiguity: Semantic Competition in Lexical Access.* **Jennifer Rodd,Gareth Gaskell and William Marslen-Wilson.** 2002, Journal of Memory and Language, Vol. 46.

59. *Libet's Timing of Mental Events: Commentary on the Commentaries.* **Stanley Klein.** 2002, Consciousness and Cognition.

60. *Left posterior auditory-related cortices participate both in speech perception and speech production: Neural overlap revealed by fMRI.* **Kayoko Okada and Gregory Hickok.** 2006, Brain and Language, Vol. 98.

61. *Learning-induced neural plasticity of speech processing before birth.* **Eino Partanen et.al.** July 2013, PNAS Early Edition.

62. *Learning in a Simple Motor System.* **Dianne M. Broussard and Charles D. Kassardjian.** 2004, Learning & Memory, Vol. 11.

63. *Language systems in normal and aphasic human subjects: functional imaging studies and inferences from animal studies.* **Richard J S Wise.** 2003, British Medical Bulletin, Vol. 65.

64. *Is neural development darwinian?* **Dale Purves, Leonard E. White and David R. Riddle.** 1996, Trends Neurosci., Vol. 19.

65. *IN THE THEATRE OF CONSCIOUSNESS: Global Workspace Theory,A Rigorous Scientific Theory of Consciousness.* **Bernard J. Baars.** 4, 1997, Journal of Consciousness Studies, Vol. 4.

66. *Imaging neural signatures of consciousness: 'What', 'When', 'Where' and 'How' does it work?* **C. Sergent, L. Naccache.** 2012, Archives Italiennes de Biologie, Vol. 150.

67. *How Self-Initiated Memorized Movements Become Automatic: A Functional MRI Study.* **Tao Wu, Kenji Kansaku, and Mark Hallett.** November 2003, J Neurophysiol, Vol. 91.

68. *How conscious experience and working memory interact.* **Bernard J. Baars and Stan Franklin.** TRENDS in Cognitive Sciences.

69. **Tappenberg, Thomas P.** *Fundamentals of Computational Neuroscience.* s.l. : Oxford University Press.

70. *Functional organisation of the neural language system: Dorsal and ventral pathways are critical for syntax.* **John D. Griffiths et.al.** 23, January 2013, Cereb Cortex., Vol. 1.

71. *Functional Anatomic Models of Language: Assembling the Pieces.* **Dorit Ben Shalom and David Poeppel.** 2008, Neuroscientist, Vol. 14.

72. *Exercising Your Brain: A Review of Human Brain Plasticity and Training-Induced Learning.* **C. S. Green and D. Bavelier.** 4, December 2008, Psychol Aging., Vol. 23.

73. *Dorsal and ventral streams: a framework for understanding aspects of the functional anatomy of language.* **Gregory Hickok,, David Poeppel.** 2004, Cognition, Vol. 92.

74. *Distinguishable Brain Activation Networks for Short- and Long-Term Motor Skill Learning.* **A. Floyer-Lea and P. M. Matthews.** February 2005, J Neurophysiol, Vol. 94.

75. *Distinct contribution of the cortico-striatal and cortico-cerebellar systems to motor skill learning.* **Julien Doyon et.al.** 2003, Neuropsychologia, Vol. 41.

76. *Defining the cortical visual systems : "What" , "Where" and "How".* **Sarah H. Creem and Dennis R. Proffitt.** 2001, Acta Psychologica, Vol. 107.

77. *Cortical mechanisms of action selection: the affordance competition hypothesis.* **Paul Cisek.** Aprill 2007, Phil. Trans. R. Soc. B, Vol. 362.

78. *Converging Language Streams in the Human Temporal Lobe.* **Galina Spitsyna, Jane E. Warren, Sophie K. Scott, Federico E. Turkheimer, and Richard J. S. Wise.** 26, July 2006, The Journal of Neuroscience, Vol. 28.

79. *Consensus Paper: The Cerebellum's Role in Movement and Cognition.* **Leonard F. Koziol et.al.** August 2013, Cerebellum.

80. *Consensus Paper: Roles of the Cerebellum in Motor Control—The Diversity of Ideas on Cerebellar Involvement in Movement.* **Mario Manto et.al.** 2012, Cerebellum.

81. *Consciousness: converging insights from connectionist modeling and neuroscience.* **Tiago V. Maia and Axel Cleeremans.** 8, August 2005, TRENDS in Cognitive Sciences, Vol. 9.

82. **RobinH, JWSchmidt and Shamantics.** *Consciousness Studies.* s.l. : A Wikibook, 2007.

83. **P., Cisek, T., Drew and F., Kalaska J., [ed.].** *Computational Neuroscience. Theoretical Insights into Brain Function.* 2007. Vol. 165.

84. *Competitive mechanisms in sentence processing: Common and distinct production and reading comprehension networks linked to the prefrontal cortex.* **Gina F. Humphreys , Silvia P. Gennari.** 2014, NeuroImage, Vol. 84.

85. *Cognitive Neuroscience and study of Memory.* **Milner, Brenda, Squire, Larry R. and Kandel, Eric R.** March 1998, Neuron Vol. 20.

86. *Change blindness: Past, present, and future.* **Daniel J. Simon1 and Ronald A. Rensink.** 1, January 2005, Trends in Cognitive Sciences, Vol. 9.

87. *Cerebellar Plasticity and the Automation of First-Order Rules.* **Joshua H. Balsters and Narender Ramnani.** 6, February 2011, The Journal of Neuroscience, Vol. 31.

88. *Central mechanisms of motor skill learning.* **Okihide Hikosaka, Kae Nakamura, Katsuyuki Sakai, Hiroyuki Nakahara.** March 2002, Current Opinion in Neurobiology.

89. *Brain Facts : A PRIMER ON THE BRAIN AND NERVOUS SYSTEM.* s.l. : Society for Neuroscience, 2008.

90. *Biology of consciousness.* **Gerald M. Edelman, Joseph A. Gally and Bernard J. Baars.** January 2011, frontiers in Psychology, Vol. 2.

91. *Behavioral semantics of learning and crossmodal processing in auditory cortex: The semantic processor concept.* **Henning Scheich et.al.** 2011, Hearing Research, Vol. 271.

92. *Basal Ganglia Contributions to Motor Control: A Vigorous Tutor.* **Robert S. Turner and Michel Desmurget.** 6, December 2010, Curr Opin Neurobiol., Vol. 20.

93. **Dirk B. Walther and Christof Koch.** Attention in hierarchical models of object recognition. *Progress in Brain Research.* 2007, Vol. 165.

94. *Apraxia, metaphor and mirror neurons.* **Editorial.** 2007, Medical Hypotheses.

95. *An Introduction to the Physics of Magnetic Resonance Imaging.* **Stephen Baiter.** 2, March 1987, RadioGraphics, Vol. 7.

96. *An evolving view of duplex vision: separate but interacting cortical pathways for perception and action.* **Melvyn A Goodale and David A Westwood.** 2004, Current Opinion in Neurobiology, Vol. 14.

97. *An emerging molecular and cellular framework for memory processing by the hippocampus.* **Gayle M. Wittenberg and Joe Z. Tsien.** 10, October 2002, TRENDS in Neurosciences, Vol. 25.

98. *Amygdala Modulation of Memory Consolidation: Interaction with Other Brain Systems.* **James L. McGaugh, Christa K. McIntyre, and Ann E. Power.** 2002, Neurobiology of Learning and Memory, Vol. 78.

99. **Thomas Serre et.al.** A quantitative theory of immediate visual recognition. *Progress in Brain Research.* 2007, Vol. 165.

100. *A neuronal network model linking subjective reports and objective physiological data during conscious perception.* **Stanislas Dehaene, Claire Sergent, and Jean-Pierre Changeux.** 14, July 2003, PNAS, Vol. 100.

101. **Elizabeth Hume and Keith Johnson.** A Model of the Interplay of Speech Perception and Phonology. *The Role of Speech Perception in Phonology.* 2001.

102. *Brain functional integration decreases during propofol-induced loss of consciousness.* **Jessica Schrouff et.al.** 2011, NeuroImage, Vol. 57.

103. *Phantom limbs and neural plasticity.* **VS Ramachandran et.al.** 2000, Arch Neurol, Vol. 57.

Image credits

- Figures 2.2, 2.3, 2.4, 2.5, 6.1, 6.2, 6.3, 6.4, 6.5, 7.1, 7.3, 7.4, 9.5, 10.4, 10.5, 12.5 use images downloaded from *Wikimedia Commons* repository and these images may be covered by appropriate licenses.

- Figures 5.1 and 7.2 are based on illustrations given in *"Brain Facts : A Primer on the brain and nervous system"*.

Thank you for reading my book. I hope you enjoyed reading it. Please give me your feedback through book reviews. I appreciate that very much. You may contact me through my blog at http://doctor-king-online.blogspot.com I will be happy to hear from you. If you have any specific questions or suggestions, indicate them through my blog and I will surely respond to them.

You may also be interested in reading my other books available through several online vendors.

My recent Books

Following is the list of my recent books. Some of these books are now available from one or more of online bookstores such as

Amazon, Scribd, Smashwords, Apple iBookstores, Barnes & Noble, Sony, Kobo, Flipkart Diesel eBook Store, eBooks Eros, Baker & Taylor, Page Foundry ,WH Smith in the UK, FNAC in France and Portugul, Livraria Cultura in Brazil, Angus & Robertson in Australia, Bookworld in Australia, Indigo in Canada, Collins in Australia, Feltrinelli in Italy, Libris in the Netherlands, Paper Plus in New Zealand, Play in Great Britain, Rakuten in Japan, Rakuten in the US, Whitcoulls in New Zealand.

Please look for them in your favorite book store. You can always use the book title in your search to see if the book is available in your favorite bookstore. I have given the appropriate links for your convenience in my blog http://doctor-king-online.blogspot.com

How does the Mind work? (Marvels of the mind Part I)

Book synopsis: The mind is probably the most complex of the nature's creations. It is an extremely fascinating and intriguing entity, probably beyond the reach of human beings to have a complete understanding.

This is the first part of a 3 part series namely *Marvels of the Mind,* discussing various aspects of the mind. While the second and third parts of this series cover philosophic and spiritual facets of the mind, this part focuses mainly on the current scientific views about how the mind functions.

While several books that explain various aspects of this wonderful subject do exist, the subject is too specialized and beyond the grasp of general readers. The technical jargon used in these books needs proper background. Besides, books often don't give up-to-date information that can only be found in research journals and conference proceedings.

Most readers may neither have access to these books or journals, nor have the necessary background to follow intense technical literature. The current book tries to overcome some of these problems by explaining this subject in an easy to understand style with lot of simple day-to-day examples. The book follows a structured approach to cater for the needs of readers with varying backgrounds and interests. The reader can pick and choose the detail depending on the interest and aptitude.

Apart from providing the readers with the latest scientific information about the functioning of the mind, the book lays the foundation for the discussion in later parts of this series about the working of Yoga and Meditation.

Important missing dimensions in our current understanding of the Mind (Marvels of the mind Part II)

Book synopsis: Our current scientific achievements in understanding the working of the mind are commendable. However, in it's over insistence on objectivity science seems to have overlooked some important dimensions of the mind. There are many questions science fails to provide satisfactory answer.

Interestingly, many of these questions were addressed by ancient philosophies and probably in the true scientific spirit we should look at these philosophies with an open mind.

This second part of the 3 part series **Marvels of the Mind** focuses on these missed dimensions and how ancient philosophies address them. A range of ancient philosophies, amazingly well conceptualized, that look at different aspects of the mind are discussed in the current book.

There is the ancient philosophy of Plato who points out the limitations of our sense perception, the elaborate psychology of ancient Buddhists that almost parallels with our scientific understanding, the philosophy of Šankara who even questions the reality of existence and the concept of domains beyond mind that are the focus of ancient Upanishads. All these, and more, are explained clearly in this second part of the series.

These philosophies compel us to rethink on our current definition of science and its approach. The book also provides a smooth transition point from science to philosophy and finally to domains beyond both these.

How and Why of Yoga and Meditation (Marvels of the mind Part III)

 Book synopsis: This book gives a clear insight into various aspects of Yoga, while providing scientifically backed explanation about how various Yoga processes achieve their intended purposes and why they are designed that way. Such clarity is needed to understand Yoga in a more scientific manner and to realize its full potential.

The book also explains in a step by step manner how various processes of Yoga, namely the body postures, breathing techniques and meditation are performed and why each of these processes is essential to attain complete benefit of Yoga.

This book is a good guide for anyone who wants to practice Yoga.

Yöga Facts: Answers to some important questions about Yöga

 Book synopsis: Going by the large number of books on Yoga that are published and sold both through printed as well as electronic media, this ancient science seems to be very popular. While various things are propagated in the name of Yoga, there is often mismatch between expectations and achievements.

This short set of questions and answers clears some of the misconceptions about Yoga by drawing attention to the original works on Yoga dating back more than 2000 years. Questions that often arise as a result of commercially motivated propaganda are answered in a matter of fact manner. At the same time, this book reassures a sincere Yoga practitioner, that the goal is not only achievable but worth the effort.

Some of the questions discussed include - controversies due to adverse scientific findings about Yoga, why many people fail to achieve any progress in spite of sincere efforts, and so on.

Psychology behind Yoga: Lesser known insights into the ancient science of Yoga

Book synopsis: Though Yöga is well known as a process to achieve the ultimate realization, not much attention is paid to its psychological underpinnings. This book builds up the theory behind Yoga based on descriptions given in ancient texts such as Yoga sutra of Patanjali (~200 B.C.) and Sänkhya Kärika of Isvara Krshna (~300 A.D.). This understanding is essential to get a complete grasp of the Yöga process.

This book clearly explains the concept of mind as defined in Yoga Sutra and Sänkhya Kärika, various states this mind can be in, and how by a step by step process the mind can be nudged into the ultimate desirable state namely the Samadhi. It discusses various hindrances one encounters while going through this process as well as how these can be overcome. As often mistaken, samädhi is not a single state but a series of progressive states one goes through as one progresses into the Yoga practice. This book explains those stages both with reference to the original sources as well as through simple analogies.

The ultimate state of Yoga, namely the niruddha state of mind is also very well explained, its implications and what exactly happens in that stage.

Ancient wisdom – Modern viewpoints: Interesting picks from ancient Indian scriptures

Book synopsis: This book captures the essence of ancient Indian scriptures, analyzing them from today's point of view. The scriptures selected are mainly the eleven Upanishads (parts of Vedic literature), Bhagavad Geetha (most important book of Indian philosophy) and the Manu Smrthi (one of the most ancient law books by Manu). All these scriptures were composed more than 2500 years ago and influence the Indian way of life even to this day. In addition to these primary scriptures, this book also cross references several other ancient Indian scriptures such as Yoga Sutra of Patanjali, Sänkhya Kärika, Närada Bhakti sutra, and Dammapada.

Some of the key aspects of each of these three main scriptures – Upanishads, Bhagavad Geetha and Manu Smrthi - are picked and presented in 6 short, crisp articles. While writing these articles, the original Sanskrit texts are relied upon with minimal re-interpretation. Adequate references to the original Sanskrit verses are given in most places, to impart authenticity to the rendering. To help the readers who may not be familiar with Sanskrit, simple English translations of these verses are also provided.

This is an ideal book for anyone who wants to have a quick overview of most of the ancient Indian scriptures. The book gives a wealth of information and surely a key to the treasure of ancient Indian scriptures.

Around the Mind

Book synopsis: Mind may probably be the most intriguing thing that has fascinated human beings, philosophers as well as the scientists, for thousands of years. This book summarizes our current scientific views on the Mind, the questions that arise due to that view, the efforts by ancient philosophies to address these questions and probably a possibility of going beyond the realms of current scientific approach.

A Mantra to enhance your mental capabilities

Book synopsis: For thousands of years, millions of people have taken advantage of one mantra which is believed to enhance the mental capabilities. Though it is used even today, it has become a prerogative of a small minority of people and seems to be going into the oblivion. The ravages of time has seriously rendered this potent mantra into an article of religious faith and deep rooted superstition, depriving the vast majority from realizing its benefits.

This book opens up this mantra to all those who are desirous of enhancing their mental capabilities. It discusses various aspects of this mantra and explains in a step by step fashion how anyone can take advantage of this mantra.